BEDDGELERT, GWYNEDD ; J CAMPBELL KERR

£4.99

KU-757-172

People's Friend

Contents

Complete Stories

p106

Dear Reader,

Happy New Year! As we enter a new century, it's good to know that some things will never change. As always, the "Friend" Annual is packed with great reading, including more than 20 new Stories to entertain and touch your heart.

As we all celebrate the millennium, we take a fascinating look back at the 20th century and the events and discoveries which have changed all our lives.

John Taylor invites us to join him on the Riggin, and popular poet Brenda G. Macrow shares her dreams of Scotland. And there are colourful paintings by "Friend" cover artist J. Campbell Kerr throughout the Annual.

With so much to enjoy, this year's Annual promises you hours and hours of great reading!

The Editor

p115

Annual 2000

p18

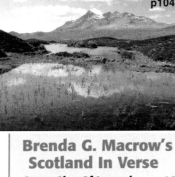

p26

p104

p88

The Farmer And His Wife
by John Taylor

p10

Illustration by Melvyn Warren-Smith.

On With

by Margaret Kingsley

LIZ PARDOE relaxed as she watched Rory starting to build his first-ever sandcastle.

On this, the first day of their holiday, the sun was climbing in a cloudless sky, the beach was beginning to shimmer, and the waves lapped lazily at the nearby breakwater.

Contentedly, Liz looked around her. The beach at White Bay was certainly a children's paradise, with its clean sand, gently shelving beach and shallow rock pools. There was even a Punch and Judy show!

She watched her six-year-old son digging a "moat" with great enthusiasm. Already he seemed to have thrown off the exhaustion which had led their family doctor to suggest a seaside holiday.

"The boy's caught every bug going over the last year. He'd benefit from a good month of sea air," he'd said some weeks ago.

After which he'd looked at Liz with some concern.

"And so would you, my dear. How are you coping without Steve?"

"We're doing fine. The divorce comes through in September."

he Show!

Her voice had held no emotion, but she knew the doctor hadn't been fooled. She still hurt badly.

"Then get away and have some fun," he'd advised. "For both your sakes."

A van coming to rest at the edge of the dunes disturbed her thoughts. She turned to see a middle-aged couple and a young man open its back doors.

The two men carried out a gaily-painted theatre booth on to the beach. The grey-haired woman followed with a basket full of props.

All three disappeared behind the booth and five minutes later a hand stretched from a side entrance to plunge a long pole, topped with a notice, into the sand.

PUNCH AND JUDY.
THE FIRST SHOW COMMENCES AT 11 a.m.

"Mum!" Rory yelled excitedly, catching the mood. "Can we go and see?"

He was off without waiting for a reply. Liz followed. In no time at all a large audience was sitting on the sand, waiting for the morning performance to begin.

At exactly eleven o'clock, the curtains on the booth drew back and Mr Punch was revealed.

"Hello, children!" His famous strangled tones carried well.

"Hello-o-o, Mr Punch-ch-ch!" the children yelled back as one voice.

OVER the years in White Bay, Bill Huddle, the latest in a long line of family presenters, had developed storylines in which Mr Punch was noisy, naughty, and argumentative — but never violent.

The grotesque little figure, dressed in red and green silk, wielded his truncheon furiously but hit no-one, except himself.

When Bill laid down Mr Punch to take his own bow, flanked by his wife and the young man, he made what Liz, and every other grown-up present, soon realised was an unexpected speech.

"Today I want to pay tribute to my wife, Jemima, for all the years she has put up with me and Mr Punch.

"The Little Fellow would not be a part of my world — or yours — if it were not for her. I'm sure you will join me in saying thank you to her."

His right hand still holding his wife's, as though he never wanted to let it go, he waited until the enthusiastic applause died down. Then he turned to the young man whose arm he was clutching as though to keep him from running away.

"I'd also like to introduce my nephew, Richard Drew. Richard is a computer analyst and he's joining the London branch of his firm in September, but he's come to help us until then. Jemima and I think he's a grand lad — and I'm sure the Little Fellow does, too!"

A burst of laughter followed by another bout of enthusiastic clapping made Richard smile weakly. He looked shy and embarrassed.

He was a good-looking man, with dark, smooth hair and wide, deep-set eyes. He was tall, too, and held himself well.

Liz suddenly realised that the unconscious intensity of her gaze had caught his attention. Now he was returning it — with interest.

She felt the colour come into her cheeks and, getting up from her place behind Rory, she walked back to where she'd left her things.

Liz was so flustered that it was a little while before she looked to see if Rory was following her. He wasn't. Alarmed, she scanned the beach.

He was up on the dunes, talking to Bill and Jemima Huddle as they shut the doors of the van. Liz scrambled to her feet and was about to hurry across, when a deep, attractive voice stopped her.

"Don't worry. Your little boy's not being a nuisance. My uncle and aunt are used to children's questions."

The speaker was a smiling Richard Drew.

"He ran across to us after you left. I realised you thought he was following you, so I decided to let you know . . ."

"That's very kind of you!" Liz felt stupid and uncertain under his smiling scrutiny. Any sympathy she initially felt for him was fading fast.

"Please don't let me hold you back," she said stiffly. "Mr and Mrs Huddle look ready to go."

He glanced towards the dunes, and grinned.

"Bye for now!" And with that he was off, making for the van.

He and Rory looked to be on a collision course — one going, one coming — until Richard took evading action and tousled the boy's hair as they passed each other.

Rory gave a shout of laughter and tried to catch at Richard's flapping shirt, but failed.

"Mum, can we eat now?" He was still laughing when he arrived by Liz's side. "I'm starving."

While they ate, Rory told her about the Huddles.

"Mr Huddle, he used to make all the puppets himself, but Richard is going to make them now, 'cos Mr Huddle's hands are too stiff. Mrs Huddle makes the clothes. I think they're all very clever, don't you, Mum?"

"Very clever," Liz agreed.

* * * *

The next two days closely followed the pattern of the first. The sun climbed a cloudless sky, the sea sparkled its way up and down the beach, and the little theatre booth gave its two performances to an enthusiastic and vociferous audience.

The Summons

by John Taylor

NOBODY can accuse me of being finicky when it comes to my food. I don't think I've ever said I didn't like what Anne has put before me over the last 60 years!

So, what got me on to this theme?

Anne and I were going up north to our daughter and son-in-law's farm and we called in at a supermarket in Perth on the way.

I was looking at the paper and magazine racks when I noticed one of my favourite farming papers, so I bought it.

Of course, when we got back to the Riggin, Anne got to it first. She wanted to read the women's page.

There was a "Recipe Of The Week".

"John, here's just the bun for your tea." Then she laughed.

"It's carrot and caraway buns."

I had to laugh, too, as I knew full well what she was getting at.

After tea, we settled down to chat about the first time I tried caraway — one Sunday afternoon in 1934!

Anne had a maiden aunt who lived in St Andrews "with a maid".

One day, she received a letter from this good lady, saying she had heard Anne had been seen with a boy from Crail. Would she bring him for tea on Sunday?

When Anne told me about the letter, I told her I couldn't go. I wouldn't be able to get back home to help with the milking and then get to church that evening.

Anne said it was a summons — I would have to go and forget church.

At three o'clock that Sunday, the maid opened the door to us. She knocked on a door and waited for the

Rory made his after-performance visits to the Huddles and their nephew, after which Richard Drew came over to speak to Liz.

He must, she told herself, have a very high opinion of himself if the coolness of her greeting and her abrupt replies didn't make him aware of her indifference to him.

But on the fourth day of their holiday things changed, though not in the way Liz could have anticipated . . .

The afternoon performance by Mr Punch and his companions had finished, Richard and Rory had made their respective visits and Liz was settling to read her book again.

"Mum!" Rory yelled. "The sand won't stay still long enough for me to make the castle walls!"

Liz dropped to her knees beside him.

"Let's see if I can help."

Together, they bent their heads over the sandcastle but it tumbled inward, no matter what they did. Rory's frustration increased.

"You've made the sand too wet." A deeper voice broke into their concentration. "Here, let me show you."

Richard Drew appeared, out of nowhere, to kneel on the other side of Rory.

Liz glanced toward the dunes. There was no van; it had gone without him.

10

command to enter.

Blow me, as she held the door open, she announced us by name!

THE aunt rose in regal fashion from her winged chair and held out a hand.

The maid then brought in a tea trolley — silver teapot, water jug and sugar basin, plus a plate of wee sandwiches, scones and a large round cake.

The tea tasted as though it had been made over a smoky Scout's fire in a tin can. How was I to know it was China tea?

Then I was handed a large wedge of the cake on a plate. I took a bite and was nearly sick.

Just at that point, the aunt bent over to poke the fire.

Well, that piece of cake went into my pocket, regardless of it being my best suit. Anne's aunt was never any the wiser.

But that's why Anne laughed when she saw the recipe for the carrot and caraway buns. Caraway is the one flavour I just can't abide!

The Farmer And His Wife

She watched silently as Richard took over, coaxing the sand to stay in place until the sandcastle started to take shape.

The man and the boy laughed and chatted together as they worked, and Liz began to feel excluded.

"We have to go now, Rory," she said. "Say goodbye to Mr Drew and help me pack our bag."

"Aw, Mum!" Rory was clearly reluctant. "Do we have to? Richard was just going to show me . . ."

Liz cast about her desperately for an excuse, and found it as a small stray cloud crossed the sun and the beach was momentarily shadowed.

"The weather looks as if it's changing. Let's go, Rory."

Richard Drew watched silently as Rory reluctantly gathered up his bucket and spade.

"Will you be here tomorrow?" the little boy asked quietly.

"I don't see why not!"

"Promise?"

"Cross my heart . . ." Richard spoke with a gentleness worthy of Bill Huddle himself.

Liz nodded briefly in his direction, then she and Rory set off towards the hotel. Though she didn't look back, she felt Richard watching them go.

"Mum —?" The hotel was just a few minutes away when Rory

spoke. "I told Mr and Mrs Huddle and Richard today about Daddy going away. Do you mind?"

Liz stopped in her tracks, seeing Rory's bottom lip quivering slightly as he looked at her.

"Richard asked where Daddy was, so I told them I didn't know. I said you were getting a divorce soon."

His lip was now quivering dangerously and Liz dropped her beach bag and held him close.

"Are you angry at me?" His voice was muffled against her.

"I couldn't ever be really angry with you, Rory." She was filled with a fierce, protective love for this young son who had never known a proper, caring father.

THAT night Liz lay sleepless for a long time, staring into the darkness. She had wanted this holiday to be a complete break, to help her over the ending of her marriage.

But Fate seemed to be conspiring against her. Time and again, she was being forced to remember the hurt . . .

She could still recall every detail of the afternoon she and Rory had returned home to find Steve gone. He'd taken all his clothes and personal effects, and left her a note, explaining why he felt the marriage was a failure.

Liz turned restlessly. Things could have been worse. Steve, at least, hadn't been mean with money, or fought for custody of Rory.

The little boy had cried when she'd told him his father wouldn't be coming back, but he'd soon recovered and adapted well. Now she only had her own emotions to deal with . . .

When Rory woke her in the morning, the sun was back climbing the sky and the air was clear and warm. He whooped with joy as he got ready for breakfast.

"Aren't we lucky, Mum! We can see Punch an' Judy again today, two times!"

Liz collected their packed lunch and they made their way to the beach.

Digging busily, Rory kept an eye out for the Huddles' van.

It was almost eleven o'clock when he ran up to Liz.

"Mum, where's Mr Punch?" he asked anxiously. "He should be here by now."

"He's probably been delayed." Liz glanced at her watch.

But as time went on, the van still didn't appear.

"Where is Mr Punch, Mum?" Rory asked for the umpteenth time.

"He's taken the morning off," Liz improvised. "I'm sure he'll be along this afternoon."

"Can we look in the rock pools while we wait for Mr Punch?" Rory brightened. "We might see a crab."

They did. A very small crab in a small, shallow rock pool full of seaweed.

Rory gave a snort of laughter.

"He's hiding from me!"

The sound of a car engine made him look up. The crab forgotten, he raced back along the beach, shouting.

"Mum, Mr Punch is here!"

Liz followed him slowly.

The van was up on the dunes but no-one was getting out. Rory stood on tiptoe at the driver's side, his voice carrying back to Liz.

"Richard! Why are you all by yourself?"

Richard got out and bent down to speak to him.

Then Rory flew back to Liz.

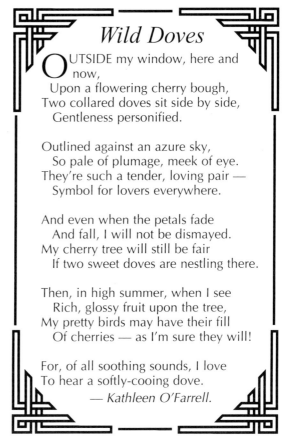

Wild Doves

OUTSIDE my window, here and
　now,
Upon a flowering cherry bough,
Two collared doves sit side by side,
　Gentleness personified.

Outlined against an azure sky,
　So pale of plumage, meek of eye.
They're such a tender, loving pair —
　Symbol for lovers everywhere.

And even when the petals fade
　And fall, I will not be dismayed.
My cherry tree will still be fair
　If two sweet doves are nestling there.

Then, in high summer, when I see
　Rich, glossy fruit upon the tree,
My pretty birds may have their fill
　Of cherries — as I'm sure they will!

For, of all soothing sounds, I love
To hear a softly-cooing dove.
　　— *Kathleen O'Farrell.*

"Mr Huddle's sick, Mum. He's in hos . . . hosp'tal. He's going to be all right, but he has to stay there for a while, and Mrs Huddle's staying with him."

When Liz looked up, Richard was putting up a notice. Then, with a wave in Rory and Liz's direction, he got back in the van and drove away.

The notice apologised for the day's absence, and said that performances would commence again tomorrow morning at the usual time. It was signed simply *Mr Punch.*

"Who's going to be Mr Punch?" Rory asked Liz after she had read the notice out loud.

"Perhaps it's a friend of Mr Huddle's!" Liz suggested.

The haze was lifting next morning when they reached their place on the beach. When the van came into sight, Rory got up and raced across to it.

Liz saw Richard get out, open the back doors, draw out the theatre

13

booth and carry it down to the beach.

Rory followed, dragging the props basket.

They both disappeared inside the booth and the sides began to bulge and shake.

At a quarter to eleven Rory came out and sat in his usual place in front of Liz. The audience seemed larger than usual and an air of anticipation grew in intensity as the moments passed.

"Where's the new Mr Punch?" Liz asked. "I haven't seen him arrive yet."

"Richard's doing it," Rory hissed.

"Richard?" She couldn't hide her disbelief.

Rory hurriedly shushed her and spoke out of the corner of his mouth.

"He doesn't want anybody to know until it's over. He learned the words last night, so he knows the story an' everything. He'll be good, Mum. I know he will."

A T exactly eleven o'clock the curtains parted to reveal Mr Punch. Today he sat quietly, looking straight ahead. There was no stick, no tension. He didn't speak.

The audience became restless as the Little Fellow's silence continued.

"Wake up, Mr Punch!" a voice shouted.

"Hello, children!" A strangled voice spoke the famous opening words.

"Hello-o-o, Mr Punch-ch-ch!" the roar came back.

But what a disaster it was!

Richard forgot his lines, forgot to move Mr Punch, ignored the baby and even, at one important point, the policeman. He muddled his words, the scenes, and the props. It was the most dreadful and embarrassing performance ever.

At the end there was no clapping, no cheering, no calls for Mr Punch to take a bow.

Richard remained within the booth until the audience had dispersed. Then he began to pack everything up and load the van.

That was when Rory and Liz went to look for him. Rory because he thought of Richard as his friend, and Liz because she told herself that she didn't want her son to have to face him alone.

They found Richard sitting on the stubbly grass with his head in his hands. He knew they were there, but he didn't look up. He cut such a miserable, dejected figure that Liz hardly recognised him.

"I made a mess of it, didn't I, Rory?" he said at last, passing a hand over his dark hair.

"I was sure I could do it. I practised all last evening until I was word perfect.

"But as soon as I opened the curtains, the thought of all those people out there, waiting for me to speak, was too much . . ." He shuddered, remembering.

"I only wanted to help, but when it came to the crunch, I froze . . ." His voice died away. Although he still didn't look at her, Liz knew he had been talking to her. He'd wanted her to understand . . .

Richard might be confident in his work with computers, but when it came to Punch and Judy, and his personal life, he had a lot to learn.

Suddenly, with an almost breathtaking clarity, she was seeing him as he really was; an ordinary, very vulnerable man — even likeable and approachable. Maybe even someone to . . .

Her thoughts stopped there. She had no desire to rush into another relationship . . .

But the fact she'd even thought of it must mean her confidence — so badly dented by Steve — was returning. For the first time, she found herself wondering if it had been anything more than her pride that had been hurt by his going. Hadn't her marriage been over long before she and Steve had parted? Hadn't she just been trying to keep it alive for Rory's sake . . .?

Liz came out of her thoughts as Rory touched Richard's arm.

"You can do it, Richard, I know you can. You just need to practise.

"I know all the words an' I know what Mr Punch an' the others have to do, so I can help you. You've got to try again. Please?"

It was the oddest of situations, Liz was to think often in the days ahead. Whoever heard of a six-year-old boy teaching a twenty-eight-year-old man how to face an audience and conquer his nerves and shyness?

Yet it happened. And she helped.

"Please — let Rory help you," she told Richard. "He really is very good at remembering the story."

He raised his head to search her face for any hidden sarcasm. There was none. She really meant what she said. It brought him to his feet.

"Why not?" He spoke with just a hint of the brash self-confidence of old. "I've nothing to lose and maybe a great deal to gain. You can teach me all you know, Rory. I promise I'll learn fast."

Liz smiled at him. She was a learner, too — learning to live again, to trust again.

No-one could be sure of the future. But for good or ill, Richard seemed to be in theirs — at least for the present.

"Mum, why don't we all go back to the hotel an' have tea?" Rory suggested.

"Why not?" Unconsciously she echoed Richard's words of a few moments ago.

And as she did so she smiled at them both. She had nothing to lose — and maybe a great deal to gain. ❏

Glen Etive, Argyll.

Green Glen
Of Legend

THE braes are green in limpid light,
 The sun is riding high,
And crimson rhododendrons bright
 Beguile the rambler's eye.

The amber waters of the stream
 Surge down with music loud.
The Etive Herdsmen guard the glen,
 Their grey heads brushed with cloud.

The rowan flaunts her creamy lace,
 The glossy bracken shines,
And fleeting shafts of sunlight trace
 The loch amid the pines.

Old sagas echo on the breeze,
 Old tales of ancient days
When Deirdre of the Sorrows walked
 Among these flowery ways.

Green glen of legend, set apart
 'Mid grizzled mountains bare,
You weave a spell to charm the heart
 When summer's in the air!
 — *Brenda G. Macrow.*

Dennis Hardley.

MANDA paused in her walk up the hill to turn and look back at the town, which lay beneath her in the late summer sun. The little white-walled cottages clustered defensively round the harbour.

Manda's pretty young face creased into a frown as she straightened the strap of her dad's camera, which was lying uncomfortably on her shoulder, and continued up the hill.

She was nearly fifteen and, every year of her life, her family had spent their holidays here.

Friends had often asked her if she didn't fancy a change. But Manda had said no, she was perfectly happy. She didn't want a change.

by Val Bonsall

MAGIC IN THE AIR

But this year it *had* changed . . .

"But you and Grandad have *always* come with us!" she'd protested to her gran.

"Well, your grandad can't any more, can he? And I don't want to, so that's that."

Gran's voice had been sharp — it often was these days since Grandad had died.

Then Gran had seemed to realise how she sounded and had given Manda a hug.

"I just don't feel like a holiday, sweetheart," she'd whispered. "I'm not in a holiday frame of mind."

Illustration by Melvyn Warren-Smith.

"Oh," Manda said. "I understand."

And she *did* understand.

Like her mum and dad had said, they had to give Gran time.

So that was when they'd put the holiday back. They'd originally planned for the high summer — their usual time — but it was worth waiting if it meant Gran would come, too.

Then, suddenly, it was nearly time for Manda to return to school and still Gran didn't want to go anywhere with them.

They didn't really want to leave her alone but she'd insisted they booked for the first of the two weeks that remained before the new term started.

Manda had tried to talk her gran into joining them right until the last morning, but without success.

"I'll miss you!" she'd wailed.

"Of course you won't!" Gran had said. "You're growing up now — you'll be off to discos every evening!"

But Manda *was* missing her gran already, just two days into the holiday.

And Grandad, too.

Manda sighed. It was Grandad who'd first found this walk, up past the larger, more ordinary houses at the edge of the town, where sand and shell were replaced by flower and shrub. Of course, Grandad, a keen gardener, had known all the names of the plants.

Then, at the top of the hill, were the rambling roses — a whole hedge of them, seeming to stretch for ever. You could see their soft pink blaze as soon as you turned the corner.

In her mind's eye, Manda saw her grandad's face as, on their first walk up here each year, he had paused for a moment to take in their beauty.

"Magic," he'd say to her. "Look, isn't that just magic?"

Now, in spite of everything, Manda's pace quickened as she approached the corner.

But there was nothing — just the glossy green leaves — there were no flowers.

Gran's parting words to Manda on the morning they'd set off had been:

"Give my love to the roses, now!"

She'd intended to take a photo of them — that's why she'd brought her dad's camera — and send it to her gran, in place of a postcard, with the message:

"The roses send their love back!"

Manda sighed again as she realised what must have happened.

They'd delayed their holiday, hoping Gran would change her mind. And that few weeks' delay meant they were too late for the flowers. They'd bloomed in high summer and were now gone.

For a moment Manda felt like crying.

No Grandad.

No Grandma.

No roses.

THE moment passed. She was on holiday — you didn't cry on holiday.

Putting the no-longer-needed camera carefully down by her side, Manda sat on a large stone and closed her eyes against the sun, enjoying its warmth.

"Good afternoon!"

The voice that spoke had the soft local dialect.

Manda opened her eyes to see a woman about the same age as her mum cycling into the drive of a nearby house.

"Oh, hello!" She smiled.

Behind the woman, also on a bike, was a boy of around her own age.

The woman got off her bike and strode up to the front door of the house, which was already open. As she entered, Manda heard the sound of friendly voices.

The boy, too, went in briefly, then came back outside.

"You on holiday?" he called to Manda.

"That's right, yes."

He leaped over the low wall surrounding the house and came over to talk to her.

Manda learned that his name was Alex and he lived down in the town.

"My mum's visiting her friend." He pointed to the house. "And I came up with her for the ride."

"You're really lucky living somewhere like this." Manda sighed.

"Yeah," Alex said. "But at this time of the year it gets too crowded in the town! That's why I came up here with Mum today — to get away from it all for a while. And I like this hill — it's got something quite special . . ." His voice tailed off.

"It's just magic," Manda said, impulsively, to fill in the silence.

Alex looked at her for a moment. Then he nodded, and grinned.

"Yeah." He paused again. "How did *you* find it? Not many tourists come wandering up here."

"I first came with my grandad," Manda explained.

"He's that sort, you know — always looking to get off the beaten track. Or, he was."

Alex was looking at her dad's camera.

"I'm going to take some photos," she said, "for my gran."

OK, the roses weren't in flower, but she'd go ahead with her plan and send a snapshot anyway, she decided.

"If you want one with you in, I'll take it for you," Alex offered.

As she chatted easily to Alex, Manda took snaps of the rose hedge, and the view of the harbour.

Then Alex took one of her, leaving just one more left.

"Smile!" She grinned, and completed the film with a picture of Alex.

"If you take it into the chemist by the harbour before four-thirty, they'll have the prints ready for tomorrow," he told her.

Manda glanced at her watch, which her gran and grandad had bought her for her birthday last year. It was already turned four o'clock! She was amazed. The afternoon had flown past!

"Right. Thanks." She picked up her camera and headed back to the town.

She stopped on her way down and glanced back.

A figure was standing watching her. The angle of the sun made it hard to be sure, but she thought it was him.

She waved anyway.

THE next morning she went for a walk along the cliffs with her parents.

With jutting rock and sparkling sea, the scenery was far more dramatic than that around the rose hedge. But she agreed with her grandad and Alex — in its quiet way, the hill had something very special about it.

It was lunchtime by the time they got back to the town.

"I'll go and get the photos," she said to her mum.

"OK. I'll pop into the baker's. See you outside."

Manda paid for the photos and hurried along the narrow cobbled street to the old-fashioned baker's they always went to.

"Manda!"

Alex was on the other side of the road. He was with a group of friends, but he detached himself from them to wave at her.

She was on the point of crossing the road to talk to him when she heard her name again. It was her mum, outside the baker's. Suddenly, she stopped.

"Umm — hi!" she called to Alex, then hurried to join Mum.

"Have they come out well?" her mum asked, nodding at the packet of photos.

"I'm just looking now."

Manda opened the envelope and flicked through them.

"Who's that boy?" Mum asked, spotting the one she'd taken of Alex.

"He was up on the hill," Manda explained, "and we got talking. He lives here."

Back at the holiday cottage, Manda wrote her message on the back of one of the photos she'd taken of the rose hedge, and put it in an envelope addressed to her gran.

"I'll just take this to the post office," she said, as soon as they'd

A Century of Change

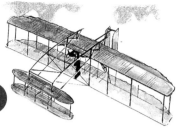

A FLYING START

WHO would have believed, at the turn of the century, that the next 100 years would bring so many changes? Nowadays we think nothing of our modern lifestyles and how easy it is to travel the globe. We take holidays abroad, never thinking, as we enjoy our flight, of the men who made it possible — Wilbur and Orville Wright. Yet it was in 1903, when their aeroplane, Flyer, took off at Kitty Hawk, North Carolina, that the era of flight really began.

The first scheduled flights from London to Paris began as early as 1919. And soon more and more routes were opening up.

It was the use of aircraft in the two World Wars which speeded the development of this form of transport. World War I saw significant advances in speed, lifting capability and reliability while, in 1944, Britain and Germany pioneered the introduction of jet engines.

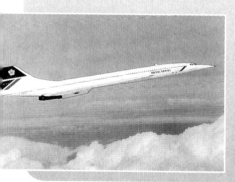

The world's first regular passenger service by a pure-jet aircraft was made in 1952 by the de Havilland Comet — flying between London and Johannesburg. Today, flights criss-cross the world and, thanks to Concorde, you can even travel faster than the speed of sound!

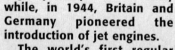

• • • • • • • • • • 1900-1909 • • • • • • • • • •

finished lunch.

After she'd posted the letter, she cut back down the street with the baker's on it, in no hurry.

A group of young people were again talking at the end. She was pretty sure it was the same group she'd seen Alex with earlier. But he was no longer with them.

She had hoped to see him today — that they could be friends while she was on holiday.

In the past, it had been Gran who'd been Manda's constant holiday

23

companion. And they'd always had such fun together.

If only Gran had come this year . . .

BOUNDING out of bed next morning, Manda opened the curtains to admire the view . . . but a sea mist had descended. Her parents — who'd planned to drive to a nearby village to re-visit its famous ancient church — were disappointed. Clearly it was not the weather to drive anywhere at all.

But Manda rather liked the mists and their concealing softness. They always gave her the feeling of a mysterious magic day — one that might be hiding surprises.

After breakfast, Manda set off to take a look in some of the town's art galleries and studios.

She stood and admired the pictures on display in the first little studio-cum-gallery she came to.

The idea of applying to art college had been attracting her for some time.

Her gran was right — she was growing up. She thought a lot these days about her life after she left school.

When she got back to the cottage, her vague thoughts about a day of surprises had taken on a reality . . .

"Your gran's coming!" Her mum greeted her. "On the train tomorrow!

"We're going to see if we can have this place for next week, too. Or somewhere else for the four of us, if it isn't free!

"She phoned your dad on his mobile phone — for once it's come in useful!" Mum laughed. "She says she's realised that . . . well, she wanted to try and enjoy life again."

Manda was as thrilled as her parents.

"I've been so worried about Mum," Manda's mum confided. "But now I think things will be all right. Oh, I wish it was tomorrow and she was here!"

"Let's take that trip to the old church we talked about earlier," Dad said. "The mist's cleared."

They were coming back, at about five o'clock, when from the car window Manda spotted Alex again.

He was alone, on his bike, coming down the road from the hill.

Perhaps he'd been visiting his mum's friend again, Manda speculated.

But she noticed that his mum wasn't with him . . .

So did that mean . . . ?

She stopped the thought almost before it had started.

For heaven's sake — she scolded herself — he could have been *anywhere!*

MANDA and her mum and dad were all there on the single platform of the little station to meet Gran. She was already looking loads better than she had for ages. And the edge that had so often recently sharpened Gran's tone was completely gone.

Manda's heart swelled with pleasure.

No mist today maybe — but it was another magic day.

"It was your photo that made me realise," Gran told Manda immediately she joined them. "Whatever happens, there are still beautiful things in life — like the roses."

She gave Manda a big hug.

"I just wish they'd been in flower," Manda began.

"What do you mean? Of course they were in flower —" Gran broke off and retrieved the photo from her handbag. "Yes, there you are."

Manda looked at the photo — the same one she herself had placed in the envelope the previous day.

And it was true — the roses *were* in bloom — a blaze of pink.

Her thoughts were interrupted again by her gran linking her arm.

"So what have you got planned for us, now I've come all this way?"

"I thought we'd go up to the hill this afternoon," Manda replied slowly. "There's someone I'd like you to meet — if he's there, of course — he might not be."

But Manda thought there was a good chance Alex would be there. That was probably where he was coming from the previous afternoon, and where he'd left his friends to go the afternoon before that.

The magic place . . . ❏

Special Day

THERE'S quite a stir within the house
    As guests arrive to stay.
A special party has been planned
    To celebrate this day.
Uncles, aunts and grandchildren,
    Friends of the family,
Are gathered all together
    In love and unity.

For it is Granny's birthday
    And she's reached eighty years.
Amidst balloons and gifts and food,
    There's laughter, smiles and tears.
A tiny, fragile lady,
    With a very agile mind,
Courageous in her spirit,
    Yet gentle, warm and kind.

She's such a caring person,
    So loving, witty, wise.
The children all adore her —
    She sees life through their eyes.
She is the guest of honour
    And, in her own quiet way,
Receives the kisses and the hugs
    Bestowed on her today.
                    — *Kathleen Gillum.*

The Girl In

THERE were so many things Greta would always remember about that day . . .

It had been uncommonly hot and humid for so early in May, especially after the week of chill easterly winds and showers they'd just had.

Caroline, her childhood friend, had suggested they ride out to the village of Little Leeham. Caroline had a car, a small grey sporty thing, very daring for a young woman in the 1950s, and she'd welcomed any opportunity to drive out into the countryside.

Greta owed Caroline so much. If her friend hadn't insisted on going out that day, all those years ago, then none of those small but hugely significant things would have happened and wisteria blue would never have come to mean so much.

Her mind wandered back and suddenly, she was there, gazing thoughtfully out over the garden when Caroline's car pulled up outside on that morning in 1954 . . .

by Jennifer List

Greta had watched unseen through the fine net curtain as her parents greeted Caroline in the front garden. As their bright, cheerful expressions changed to concern, Greta had known they were talking about her — and Ted.

Ted had been gone for a month, but the pain she'd felt that day was as acute as it had been when she'd first realised that he was gone for good.

She'd always imagined that they would marry some day; it seemed a natural progression, as day follows night and summer follows spring. Nothing was official, but there had been an unspoken understanding and their names were always mentioned as one.

Ted had told her they'd always be together, that he couldn't stand to be separated from her rosy smile and shining dark brown curls for a minute. She'd rested her head on his shoulder, allowed herself to become intoxicated on his heady aftershave and bathed in the glow of his hazel eyes.

When Ted had told her he was looking for a new job she hadn't been unduly concerned. He was an engineer, and the opportunities were numerous for someone with his talent.

Greta had sensed his excitement when he thought he'd secured a good position and didn't really wonder why he kept so many details to

isteria Blue

Illustration by Pat Gregory.

himself. She didn't press him to tell her more, never expecting the truth would be so hard to take.

As they parted that particular Friday night he'd told her of his success.

"It's a dream career," he said. "It's just what I've always wanted. The opportunities for the future are marvellous, and the wages are twice what I'm getting now.

"They want me to start as soon as I can. I've handed in my notice at work — I'm leaving England in three weeks . . ."

"What?" Greta cried. "Leaving England? Ted, what are you talking about?"

He'd lowered his eyes and forced his hands into the pockets of his coat. Then he'd lifted his head and spoken over Greta's shoulder to nowhere in particular.

"The job's in America, on the east coast. It's a chance I just can't miss. But look, I'll be home every three months. The time will soon go, you'll see. Nothing will change . . ."

Had a bolt of lightning leaped from the sky and struck her squarely in the chest, Greta could not have felt more stunned, more hurt. She could remember nothing of the hours that followed — they were just a haze.

But, gradually, three months began to seem less than a lifetime, and then, hardly any time at all. She began to toy with the idea of life in another country, until she became as excited about the future as Ted.

Their final parting had been full of hope, plans and promises. At the airport he'd dried her tears, kissed her salty cheeks and reminded her that three months was not that long.

She had found the note when she got home, addressed to her in Ted's neatly sloping handwriting. But instead of the words of love she expected, she found more pain.

He had lied. There was no three-monthly leave, and even if there were he would be spending it abroad. Ted had been unable to tell her that he was leaving his home and country — and her — for good.

She had felt bereaved, cheated, humiliated. Her future had been stolen from her, the man she'd loved and trusted had deceived her. In the next few short weeks she had fallen into a sorrow so deep that there were no colours in her life any more — only grey.

THE front room door had opened and Caroline came in. Caroline brought sunshine to every room she entered. Her dark hair with auburn highlights that caught the sun glowed healthily against the bright summery dress she wore that morning.

"Hello, Gret," she said warmly. "How are you today?"

"I'm fine," Greta replied. She smiled, but her eyes were sad.

"That's good," Caroline said, purposefully ignoring this. "Then you can get dressed up and come out with me for the day."

"Oh, I don't think —" Greta began uncertainly.

"Greta! You've got to start living again!" Caroline blurted out. She touched her friend's arm gently and her voice softened.

"I know how badly Ted hurt you . . ."

Greta turned to the window and fingered the curtain.

"He must have had good reason to leave the way he did. He obviously just couldn't face telling me in person."

"Then think," her friend urged gently, "if your love was as strong as you're remembering, he wouldn't have been able to leave. And if you'd married, how many times in the future would he 'not have been able to tell you in person'?

"He's gone, Gret. It was shameful of him to treat you like that, so now you've got to think of yourself." She pointed out of the window.

"The world is still out there, full of life and hope. Ted has chosen a place in it for himself, and done so quite selfishly. I won't stand by and see your place become one room behind these curtains.

"Now, are you coming out with me or not?"

For a moment neither had spoken.

After all this time, Greta could only now realise just how wise Caroline's words had been. She was also remembering how close she'd been at that point to closing the door against the world for good. But, instead, she'd decided to do the opposite.

"Where are we going then?" the girl in 1954 had asked, and Caroline, who must have feared she had spoken out of turn, knew she had broken through.

In the little sports car, driving along roads bordered by the first flowers of summer, Greta remembered she'd asked that same question again.

"I thought we'd drive out to Little Leeham," Caroline answered. "I haven't been there for years, and it's a nice day for tea-rooms and antique shops."

Greta agreed. She hadn't been to the village for some time herself. It was about 20 miles from their small home town on the coast, but since those Sunday afternoon outings as a child she'd never returned.

Little Leeham was really just two narrow streets which met at a market place. From there, the main street climbed tortuously up a steep hill to a magnificent Gothic church.

She took out a small compact from her handbag and glanced briefly at her face in the tiny mirror. She realised, to her surprise, that she had lost weight in the recent weeks.

She had always tended towards plumpness and frequently bemoaned her round cheeks and softly dimpled chin. But this new, thinner look didn't suit her after all, she decided.

Greta felt a sudden pang of resentment that Ted had done this to her

— had made her do this to herself. She had shut herself away too long. It was time to rejoin the world and try to build a new life.

Caroline had parked her pride and joy at the bottom of the hill and the two young women began the slow upward climb. The sultry midday heat descended. In the sheltered street the faces they passed were red and shining and many people sought shade where they could.

T HEY walked for a while and then Caroline paused in the doorway of an art gallery. Greta knew that her friend, talented artist that she was, would long to go inside whilst she wanted to climb, right up to that wonderful church.

"Look, I can tell how much you want to go in there, Caroline, so go. I'll be fine, I'd much rather stay outside. We'll just meet back here — about half past one?"

"Well, if you're sure?" Caroline replied. "I feel awful, leaving you alone like this. It wasn't the idea after all, was it?"

"Nonsense, I'm perfectly happy."

Caroline's gaze was hesitant.

"Really, I insist," Greta went on firmly. "Enjoy your art collection. I'll see you later."

She turned and strode on up the hill. Behind her, Caroline smiled, a smile that came with the certainty that Greta was going to reach the top of more than just this particular hill in time.

As yet the church was still out of sight. Greta felt suddenly and strangely free, unencumbered by the need to make small talk to anyone.

I'm almost invisible, she mused, alone in a place where I am unknown. I can shrug off memories and no-one will suspect anything. Ted doesn't exist here — he never did.

She went on, sidestepping a small child who strayed into her path. She smiled at his flustered and apologetic mother. She'd never thought of herself as a mother. She would probably have had children with Ted, she supposed . . .

Around the next corner, she was drawn to a small group standing on the edge of the pavement.

Helmsley, North Yorkshire

A NY visitor to this town will surely be charmed by its pretty red-roofed houses and old market square. Helmsley is a good base from which to explore Ryedale and the Yorkshire Moors and there are plenty of tracks and footpaths inviting the walker to discover the lush green scenery of this part of England.

Helmsley itself boasts a castle (now ruined) which is surrounded by an unusual double ditch.

HELMSLEY, NORTH YORKSHIRE : J CAMPBELL KERR

It was immediately apparent why they were so transfixed. They were looking at a building that stood out from all the rest, with gleaming white walls and striking black wrought ironwork.

From the highest point, its roots hidden somewhere below, trailed a great river of full-blossomed wisteria, its blooms hanging in breathtaking blue sprays.

When the other admirers moved on and she was alone with the spectacle, she glanced shyly around. A young man was standing opposite, and he held a camera casually in one hand, as though waiting to capture the sight for ever.

Waiting — for her to get out of the way! Oh, how clumsy of her not to be invisible when it really mattered.

She made to walk away, lifting her hand slightly and mouthing the word, 'Sorry'. But, to her surprise, the photographer came across the road towards her.

"I do apologise. I really had no idea you were waiting to take a photograph," she said simply, trying to judge the expression in his brilliant green eyes.

"No, no, don't be sorry." He laughed, and his face wrinkled into a broad, warm smile. "Actually, I have rather a strange request for you. It may well be me that's apologising in a moment!"

Greta looked at him quizzically and noticed how his mouth twitched nervously beneath a trim moustache.

"You see, I was standing over there, waiting for that group of tourists to pass by when you stopped to look at the wisteria. It's very lovely, isn't it?"

"Yes, quite the best I think I've seen," she answered politely, intrigued.

"And as you stood there, I realised that the colours of the house, the railings, the flowers — they all complement your dress so perfectly."

Greta looked down at her dress hurriedly. It was a full-skirted summer outfit, predominantly a soft powder blue with toning flecks of white and beige, pulled in to the waist with a narrow black patent belt. She laughed.

"Goodness, how right you are. I would never have noticed."

The photographer laughed with her and relaxed a little.

"What I was thinking," he went on, and his voice was quite deep and kindly, "was, I should very much like to photograph the house and the wisteria with you standing in front of it." He looked shyly at her, awaiting her reaction.

"It just made such a perfect picture — a house dressed in blue wisteria, and a girl dressed in wisteria blue." He gave a nervous chuckle.

Greta smiled.

"It's a very clever idea," she said. "I can't imagine my presence enhancing a picture, but I have no objections if that's what you want. What shall I do?" She gave him an encouraging smile.

"Oh, please just stand as you were, gazing upwards, that's all," he said excitedly.

"If you could see just how marvellous that looks from across there! I'll just be a second. Thank you so much."

With that, he dashed out across the street, narrowly avoiding a collision with a man on a bicycle. Amidst loud exclamations, the frantic ringing of the bicycle bell, and then more apologies from the photographer, Greta tried hard to hide her giggles.

She turned and self-consciously struck her pose, afraid to move and wondering how long it would take. Then she felt a light touch on her arm and he was beside her again.

"All done," he said. "And it's going to look marvellous, just perfect. I'm hoping to do this for a living, you see, and I'm trying to build a portfolio of my work. This one will bring nothing but admiration, I'm sure of that.

"Thank you again." He grasped Greta's hand firmly in his and shook it warmly. "I must let you go now, I've wasted too much of your time already."

Greta remembered saying something vague about not being in a hurry and how pleased she was to have been of assistance. She'd wished him luck in his work and then they'd said goodbye.

THE church was just as impressive as she recalled. She passed through the gates and up the narrow path to the door. But instead of going inside, she stood by the shady north face and looked down over the valley. The ancient stone was cool against her glowing back and the long grass was still damp around her ankles.

Away from the heat and the town, and with the valley stretched out before her, she felt a strange thrill inside. She realised how flattered she felt at the photographer's delight in her.

She could still feel the touch of his hand on her arm and wondered if, when he shook her hand, he hadn't held on just a second too long?

Why, she mused sadly, did she need to be alone in the shady privacy of the churchyard before her imagination dared find its wings? Did she feel deep down that she was betraying Ted and all that they'd shared by thinking of a stranger she'd never see again? It saddened her to think this might be true.

Walking back to meet Caroline, Greta found herself gazing at each tall man she passed, ready to smile, but none of them was the handsome fair-haired photographer.

Opposite the house with the wisteria she paused and looked carefully around. There was no sign of him, and she wondered with disappointment if she had imagined the whole episode. She didn't even know his name.

She arrived early at the gallery and crossed the street to look in the window of a small antiques shop. Curious, she went inside.

The shop felt cool and shady, despite being quite cramped. In one corner, behind a small counter, stood a slender woman, her coal-black hair streaked with grey. She smiled at Greta as their eyes met.

In the far corner of the shop, an archway led into an annexe and Greta made her way through.

She decided that she would like very much to buy a suitable memento of her special day. Cups and plates, ornaments and trinket boxes — there was nothing that really took her eye until, suddenly, there it was!

It was a small opaque glass vase, Victorian, she guessed, and delicately painted with a flowery spray. It was perfect, and no more so than because its creamy smooth body was wisteria blue.

OUT in the main shop, another customer had entered to escape the glare of the day. He, too, smiled at the woman with black hair and began to look around. Making his selection from a high shelf, he took it to the counter.

The woman with black hair looked at it admiringly.

"It's very lovely, isn't it? Such a beautiful colour," she said.

"That's what drew my attention, actually," the customer replied. "It reminds me of something I saw earlier."

"Do you know, I think this is one of a pair. Would you like me to find out?"

"By all means," came the reply. "Two would be even nicer."

The woman left her position in the corner and headed for the annexe.

Greta was holding the wisteria blue vase firmly in her hands. She looked up briefly as she heard a woman's voice and saw the shop owner coming towards her, talking to someone who followed a few steps behind.

"I think I saw it in here. I can't imagine how they came to be put in different places, but then these things happen, don't they?" The woman began to hunt around, and Greta looked back to her vase, ignoring the activity.

"Oh, my, there it is! I'm afraid this lady has beaten us to it," the shop owner cried.

Greta looked up swiftly as she realised the woman was talking about the vase. The customer who had followed her into the annexe appeared at her shoulder.

"Hello," the photographer said. "We meet again, so soon."

Greta gasped in surprise. Her eyes met his and he held her gaze — for just one wonderful second too long. Guilt flooded over her, as if he could tell that she had been searching for him all the way down the hill.

She forced herself to look away, look down with the modesty that

A CENTURY OF CHANGE

NOW, as we browse the supermarket shelves, or shop for a new dress in our favourite chain store, we probably don't give a thought to Henry Ford, the founder of Ford motor cars. Yet it could be argued that it was Ford's introduction of a moving assembly line at his car plant in Michigan on October 7, 1913, which began the revolution in our shopping habits.

Henry Ford's moving line greatly increased efficiency and costs were cut. So, the Model T rolled off the production line.

Applying similar techniques of mass production to their own industries meant that manufacturing in all sorts of other areas was transformed.

Off-the-peg clothes saved the housewife a great deal of work. And, in the kitchen, life was easier, too. Food processing techniques, including canning and freezing, brought an ever wider

variety of foods to our tables and many were ready to serve.

Soon, with the introduction of new materials, the quality and variety of furniture and furnishings in our homes also increased. Life was better all round!

. . . . **1910 - 1919** . . . .

was befitting. What she saw was a blue glass vase identical to her own precious one, but looking strangely smaller in his strong but gentle hands.

She looked up again.

He read her thoughts.

"It was the colour," he said simply and shrugged his broad shoulders. Neither of them noticed the shop owner slipping quietly away.

"What are we going to do?" Greta asked, nodding her head towards the vase. "They're quite clearly a matched pair."

"Oh, absolutely," he replied. "And I can see that you want that one very badly."

Greta realised she was cradling the vase tenderly, stroking it like a kitten.

"I'm afraid so." She paused. "It's the colour."

He laughed.

"But I couldn't dream of depriving you," she went on. "That wouldn't be at all fair."

He moved closer. Or did she just imagine it?

"No," he said.

"It wouldn't be right to separate them, would it?"

"Oh, absolutely not." His brow furrowed. He looked very earnest. "Things that were meant to be together should never have to be apart."

That was the moment, the moment she knew.

"Then what should we do?" she asked, and her voice was small and trembling.

"I guess we shall have to come to some sort of arrangement."

* * * *

The afternoon shadows had lengthened as the weary sun began to set. Greta looked at her watch. Heavens! How long she'd been standing there.

The children were still playing with their grandfather in the garden. The children — her children's children!

Her two sons were grown up now, both married, and fathers, too. They looked just like their father at that age, and were making their beautiful, loving wives very happy, just like she was.

Greta smiled. She must give Caroline a ring. They hadn't seen her or her husband for weeks.

It was time they came over and had lunch, maybe went out somewhere — as long as they all kept Caroline's husband away from any art galleries! Otherwise, that would be all they'd see of him for the day. And to think she'd worried that Caroline would have been waiting all by herself that day. As if!

She sat down in her chair and reached across for the telephone. Listening to the soft, purring tone as she waited for her friend to answer, her eyes wandered around the room.

There, on top of the piano, was the beautiful Victorian vase, still such a wonderful, special colour: wisteria blue. Not far away was its identical twin, the other half of the pair, together, as they'd been since an autumn day just a matter of months after their purchase on a hot May afternoon in 1954 . . . ❑

I'D seen the dark, pretty girl several times before, while walking the dog on the heath.

She was always with another guy and we'd just nod and go our separate ways. But tonight, wearing an anorak and waterproof trousers, she was sitting on a huge boulder, gazing into the pond — alone.

I stopped and stared. I suppose you might think I was being rude, but it was dusk, the rain was bucketing down, so I was a mite curious.

None of your business, Tom, I told myself, but Ben, the collie, thought otherwise. He went across to investigate.

by Barbara Dynes

Illustration by Gerard Fay.

A LEAP IN THE DARK

Dragging the muddy animal off, I apologised, then found myself asking whether she was looking for anything in particular.

"A natterjack," she shouted over the wind.

"Ah, I see," I replied, doubtfully. I think I knew it was something that hopped, but the silly side of me immediately pictured a guy called Jack who talked too much.

"It's a toad," the girl explained, somewhat scathingly. She looked up at me from under her hood, her dark eyes huge in the twilight.

"Rare, now, natterjacks. And they've been spotted out here." She peered into the murky water once more.

I blinked. Surely seeing anything at all in these conditions was debatable?

"Lovely dog! How old is he?" she asked, still concentrating.

"No idea! Ben's not mine, you see."

How could anyone call such a bedraggled object "lovely"? I, no doubt, looked even worse.

Rain dripped off my hair, nose, jacket and every other possible place and my feet felt like two rapidly defrosting frozen kippers! What a way to spend a Saturday night!

But Jane Hodges, a single mother living down the road from me, had hurt her back and I'd gallantly volunteered to walk her dog — Ben.

"It's a bit late to be out on your own," I said.

"But they come out of hiding at dusk," she answered. "And they lay their eggs in ponds.

"I'm Anna," she added. "Been coming here with Paul, but that's all over . . ."

She stopped abruptly. Her shoulders seemed to sag under the bulky anorak and I suddenly, absurdly, wanted to crouch down and put a very wet arm around her. But I just stood there, watching the rain bounce off the water.

"I'm Tom," I ventured. "I know how it feels, finishing with someone. Being divorced myself . . ." I paused. Why should my past be of any interest to a girl with a passion for toads?

"Really?" Anna murmured vaguely. "It's their yellow streak that separates them from the others."

At first I thought she meant divorced people. Was I yellow-streaked as well as mud-streaked? Then I cottoned on. She was referring to the natterjacks!

"Terrible weather for toad-spotting," I commented.

"True! But I want to be able to say that I've actually seen one," she declared. Strands of hair had escaped from under her hood. "I'm doing a wildlife slide show for children at the Town Hall tomorrow afternoon."

She glanced up at me for a second, then returned to studying the pond.

"There he is — look!" Anna suddenly whispered excitedly.

I blinked in the direction of her finger.

"Yes, I think so," I answered doubtfully, peering through the rain at something small and brown. It could just as easily have been a rat.

"See the yellow streak?" she hissed, leaning so far forward that she was in danger of joining the creature.

I was about to make a grab at the anorak when Ben, perhaps sensing something rare in the air, began to bark hysterically.

"Ben!" I yelled, as the dog made a dive for the water.

Too late!

I groaned as the pond erupted. Vast quantities of water shot up, rivalling the rain coming down. Ben got straight back out, shaking himself all over us, but, needless to say, Mr — or Mrs — Toad had hopped it.

"Anna, I'm so sorry," I said, dismayed, as I put Ben on the lead. "I had no idea —"

"Good night," she said curtly, from under the hood.

I didn't need to see her face — it was all there in her voice. Icy, like my feet.

Abandoning all thoughts of escorting Anna back across the moor, I tugged at Ben's lead and wended my miserable way alone. I'd have to go home, change and rub down the wretched dog before handing him over to Jane.

L ATER, I found .myself, somewhat reluctantly, in Jane Hodges' chaotic kitchen. In spite of my protests and her bad back, Jane, with five-year-old Ryan in tow, had insisted on making me coffee.

"Good exercise," she said.

Baffled, I thanked her — women's logic has always been beyond me!

I hardly knew Jane, though she lived just down the road. Yet, somehow, my failed marriage seemed to have reached her ears.

I followed her into the lounge where Ben, chastised and still resembling a tatty old rug, had been banished to his basket.

"Ryan, move some of that stuff!" Jane waved at the mountain of toys and sticky unmentionables occupying the settee.

The child reached out wildly and a few things crashed to the floor. He smiled triumphantly at me.

I grinned, perching myself on the edge of the settee. I like kids. They were high on the agenda had Penny and I . . .

But I didn't want to think about Penny tonight.

My mind was still very much on the natterjack girl. Call it chemistry, call it anything, but there'd been something between us . . . and I don't just mean that toad.

Then I sighed. You blew it, Tom.

Needing to talk about Anna, I rambled on about her as I drank my coffee.

Jane listened in silence. Then she frowned.

"She sounds . . . odd," she said. "Anyone who sits in the middle of the heath in this weather looking for a toad —"

"Ah, this is not just any toad! It's rare!"

"I know," Jane said. "The natterjack has a yellow stripe down its head and back. And makes a terrible racket in the mating season, I believe," she added, smiling.

"Really?" I said. Why was I so ignorant about the things?

"Ryan, that book of yours about pond life —"

"I'll get it!" he shouted and shot out of the room.

"I don't suppose I'll see Anna again." I sighed.

"Of course you will!" Jane gave me a knowing look. "And if you read up on natterjacks, you'll be bound to create a good impression!"

I shifted uneasily. Was my interest in Anna really so obvious?

"I doubt whether she'll be on the heath tomorrow." I tried to sound as though it didn't matter a jot. "She's doing this wildlife show for kids —"

"Got it!" Ryan yelled, plonking himself on my knee and opening the book.

"There's frogs, fishes, jellyfishes . . ."

For Ryan's sake, I feigned enthusiasm over pictures of the beautiful, the disgusting and the downright ugly inhabitants of ponds.

All I really wanted to do was to go home and wallow in my misery. I was pathetic! Falling for a complete stranger! I resolved to forget the whole sorry, soggy business.

"The solution's staring us in the face," Jane said suddenly.

"If you can put up with us, why don't we all go to this show tomorrow? I'm sure I could cope and Ryan would love it!"

"I do feel responsible for what happened. Maybe you and your Anna could talk?"

I had to smile. "My" Anna! Women are such romantics!

But Jane Hodges meant well and, with Ryan jumping around excitedly at the prospect, what else could I do but agree?

If Anna ignored me, so be it . . .

IGNORE me she did — at first.

OK, so she was busy sorting slides and the hall was in semi-darkness — Anna and I seemed destined to meet in the half-light — but I was sure she spotted us as we took our seats.

"She's pretty, your toad girl," Jane remarked, sitting down carefully.

I glanced furtively at Anna and took a deep breath.

In waterproofs and anorak she had looked ravishing. Today, in a white top and trousers, with her long hair tied back, she

Golden Days In Glen Shiel

THOSE were the golden days,
   The days that linger long in memory,
When we were young and free,
When there was time to laze
And watch the swallows fly
Like arrows on the cloudless summer sky.

And we remember still
A curl of mist upon a distant hill;
The turtle-dove that crooned from leafy bower,
A poppy field in flower,
And drifts of bluebells, bright as tropic seas,
Catching the light beneath the woodland trees.

And though the passing years
May bring us pain or tears,
Yet, in the heart,
We keep intact a secret place apart
Where time stands still and summer never dies —
Where, under azure skies,
We breathe again the meadow-scented air,
And, free from care,
Can listen all day long
To fluting birdcalls and the cricket's song.
— *Brenda G. Macrow.*

Dennis Hardley.

Loch Cluanie, Glen Shiel.

looked even more so.

The show was fascinating. Well, if I'm honest, fifty per cent of it was — I got a bit bored at times.

But the children loved it. Ryan sat mesmerised, clutching a picture he'd painted specially to give "the teacher" later on.

Anna left her slides of frogs and toads till last.

"Natterjacks have been legally protected in Britain since 1975," she announced. "They're quite rare now. But did you know you could find them on our own heath? I saw one yesterday, just for a second . . ."

Her voice seemed to rise an octave and I slid down in my seat, staring at the floor like a naughty schoolboy. I could hear Jane trying to muffle giggles.

I could only hope that Anna, too, would have seen the funny side of Ben's antics by now. I listened as she thanked people for coming, then wound up the show.

"I'll just let Ryan give Anna his picture, then we'll wait outside," Jane said, over the applause.

"I'll also make it clear who we are. She might think I'm your ex-wife and Ryan's your son. That would never do," she added drily.

I stopped clapping and stared at her.

Good thinking, I wanted to say, but it didn't seem right. It sounded as though I was using them.

"Jane," I began, but she was already pulling Ryan through the crowd. I followed nervously, hanging back as she spoke.

"Anna, I just wanted to apologise for my dog's behaviour last night," Jane said. "My friend, Tom, was exercising Ben for me and told me what happened —"

"That's OK! It couldn't be helped."

"I've done a picture for you!" Ryan cried excitedly, thrusting the crumpled painting of a bright red jellyfish into Anna's hands.

"Thank you," Anna murmured, but she was looking over the boy's head at me.

I smiled at her, breathing hard.

"Good, isn't it, Ryan's picture?" I said. Much as I wanted to talk to her, I didn't want to steal his thunder.

"Was the lecture OK?" Anna asked eagerly, ignoring my question. Hardly glancing at the painting, she put it on the table amongst the slides.

"Yes, fine!" I answered, aware that Jane was tactfully steering Ryan towards the door. He was still jabbering about his painting.

"You talk to the children, Anna," I urged, uneasily. "I'll see you afterwards."

Anna merely smiled the warm smile I remembered from the night before.

As I waited for it to have the same devastating effect on me, I found myself thinking about the painting that Ryan had spent all morning doing, then picturing his crestfallen face as he walked away.

Of course, I told myself, there could be all sorts of excuses for Anna's indifference. She was tired after the lecture . . . or perhaps in a rush to get away, or . . .

"Tom, I've something to tell you," Anna was saying excitedly.

I'd heard that same excitement in her voice last night when she'd spotted the natterjack. What rare being had she found this time? A greater-spotted lizard or a luminous frog?

"My ex-boyfriend, Paul, phoned last night," she exclaimed triumphantly.

I blinked, visualising a fluorescent Paul croaking down the phone.

"We're giving it another go!" Anna went on. "He's booked us in for a nature ramble next weekend. Wish me luck!"

I stood there, waiting for the grey cloud to descend once more. Nothing happened.

"Happy rambling!" I said fervently.

ANNA wasn't right for you, Tom," Jane said, in the car on the way home. "And not only because of your lack of interest in the great outdoors."

She was looking at me uncertainly, a shy but warm expression on her face.

With a jolt, I realised what those lovely grey eyes were saying and I turned back to the road before I put three lives in jeopardy.

I drove on, thinking hard. Why hadn't I recognised the rapport between myself and Jane before?

Too besotted elsewhere, of course!

Now I was feeling happier by the minute. I tried to remain cool.

"Anna seemed different today," I remarked.

Jane didn't answer.

Instinct told me that she was much too nice to say how she really felt about Anna.

It was dawning on me that, like the natterjack, Jane Hodges had a rare quality about her. A little voice suddenly piped up from the back seat.

"Uncle Tom, can I draw you a jellyfish when I get home?"

"Yes, please. I'd love one!" I declared.

I grinned at Jane.

She smiled that quiet smile of hers and I wanted to stop the car just to relish the tender look in her eyes. But time enough later for such delights.

I knew I was about to say goodbye to my quiet life. A ready-made family, plus dog, could be somewhat chaotic. But much more fun than natterjack toads.

Well, that's my opinion . . .❑

Illustration by
Melvyn Warren-Smith.

W HEN Gillian Talbot heard she was going to live in the country, she began to have the most elaborate daydreams. She'd heard so many country stories, and seen so many pictures of it, that she thought she knew all about the countryside . . .

There were lovely green fields and little cottages with thatched roofs and honeysuckle round the door. Donkeys peered over gates and little lambs played in the fields, while jolly old farmers drove along the twisting roads in bright red or yellow tractors.

The country, she decided, would be fun.

And the grandfather she'd never met before would be kind and warm hearted, with his arms wide open in welcome, a big, beaming smile on his face.

"We're going to move soon," she told her friend Susan, whose family lived next door.

"We're going to live with my grandad in the country, in a pretty house.

"There's a village down the road, and I expect it's got a village green, and a duck pond. And on May day, the morris-dancers will come and hop about and make everyone laugh, and we'll all dance around the maypole."

The Perfect Daydream

by Kathleen O'Farrell

"Fancy that!" Susan, a lot older than her friend, could have said more, but was too good natured to dampen Gillian's enthusiasm. She just wished, silently, that Gillian wasn't going so far away.

Most of the neighbours felt the same. They would all miss the Talbots, and they knew that Alan and Anita dreaded making the move. But when Alan's business had collapsed, they'd had little choice. Alan's father had offered them a home and they were grateful, though they knew things weren't going to be easy.

"Why haven't I seen Grandad before?" Gillian asked her mother as they packed some cases together. She just couldn't understand it.

45

Anita had to explain, as tactfully as she could, that Daddy and Grandad had fallen out a long time ago.

"You see, pet, Grandad had just two sons — Daddy and your Uncle Robert, who went to live in New Zealand.

"It was all right about Uncle Robert going, because he was the younger son. But Daddy was meant to stay and run the farm. Only he didn't want to. He moved to London as soon as he was old enough and got a good job . . . Your grandad never got over it."

There was a whole lot more to it than that, of course, but Anita chose her words carefully, not wanting to prejudice Gillian against her grandfather.

Life hadn't been kind to Adam Talbot . . . He was a widower now and, without a son to carry on, had sold the farm he'd once been so proud of.

Anita and Alan had tried, so many times, to make amends, but Adam had always shunned them — until now. How wonderful it would be, Anita thought longingly, if they could all forgive and forget and start again.

Her little daughter, however, was complacently confident.

"Don't worry, Mummy —" Gillian's face shone "— I expect we'll soon all be best friends. It'll be lovely to have a grandad and I'll be ever so kind to him." She sat down for a moment, cupping her chin in her hands.

"I know what I'll do — I'll knit him some bedsocks." She could see herself helping dear old Grandad along, with tender, loving care. Just like the little girl in one of her story books.

THE Talbot family moved to Pringlehill in early January, on a dark, sleety day.

Gillian stared out of the car window in shock at the black and muddy fields full of desolate-looking sheep. People scurried along lonely roads with their heads down, their faces set.

The picture-books had got it all wrong, Gillian thought unhappily, tears suddenly not far away.

"January is the worst time for seeing the country," Dad told her, seeing her downcast face. "Just you wait — it'll be nicer in the spring."

But everything was so different from Gillian's happy daydreams.

Grandad's house, to start with, though spacious and comfortable, was very modern. Where was the thatched roof, and lattice windows? And instead of a bright flower-filled garden, there were big shrubs and looming trees which seemed to close in on them as they drove up to the front door.

But Grandad was an even greater shock than the house, Gillian was soon to find out. There wasn't a hint of Father Christmas about him. He was on the right side of sixty, a rather handsome man, with a fierce, proud face, and an abrupt way of talking.

Gillian wasn't even sure she was going to like him . . .

Yet, against all the odds, they settled down within a matter of days.

Alan, a graphic designer, was lucky enough to find a job in a market town a few miles away, while Anita, a beautician, became an agent for a well-known brand of cosmetics. Gillian was very proud of her mother, who was as pretty as you could wish for, and so friendly and nice, and such a good cook as well.

Even Adam Talbot, who had once been so angry that his son had chosen a beautician in preference to a farmer's daughter, had to admit that Anita was charming — and such a good housekeeper, too.

Within a month, they'd all slipped into an easy routine.

"It's going to work, darling. It really is," Anita told her husband eagerly.

"Once we get through this dreadful winter, and the sunny days come, we'll be really happy, I'm sure of it. There's such a lot of scope in that huge garden, and I've got all sorts of plans in my head. Flowers everywhere! Your father's given me a free hand."

Alan was delighted that his wife and his father got on so well. The reconciliation with Adam had been low-key but heartfelt. And now they were all well settled together — all except Gillian.

Gillian had completely changed her mind about the country. She hated it.

W HY can't we go back to London?" she kept asking, though her parents had explained time and time again that they were in Pringlehill to stay.

Mummy reminded Gillian that she had a lovely bedroom, that Sparky the kitten was thriving, and that Grandad was really quite nice, behind his rather fierce exterior.

"I wish you'd be more friendly towards Grandad." Anita sighed.

But Gillian shrugged.

"I don't like him very much," she admitted.

How silly she'd been to think of knitting him bedsocks! It would be like knitting bedsocks for Clint Eastwood — surely they were about the same age!

"I know he seems a bit grumpy sometimes." Anita bit her lip. "But he was on his own for ages and he's not used to having a little girl in the house. That's why he tells you off sometimes. It's just his way . . ."

Gillian sighed loudly. It wasn't just at home that she was unhappy — she didn't seem to fit in at school. She still hadn't made a single friend, even though Mrs Palmer, her teacher, had tried hard to make her welcome.

Paul Halford, from the village bakery, called her "Toffee-Nosed Talbot", because, he said, she spoke so funny. While Rosemary Carter,

LOCH DIABEG, TORRIDON : J CAMPBELL KERR

Loch Diabeg, Torridon

THERE can be few more dramatic places on Scotland's west coast than Torridon. Mighty mountains tower over a blue-green sea loch dotted with islands.

It was at little Diabeg village, at the end of the narrow, twisting road which runs along the north of the loch, that "Loch Ness" was filmed. And it would be difficult to find a more romantic location!

Torridon is a Mecca for walkers and nature lovers, keen to escape to this peaceful, friendly retreat.

who sat next to her in class, made fun of her red hair.

But Gillian didn't carry tales home.

IT was one day towards the end of February when Mrs Palmer made an announcement to her class.

"Tomorrow, we're going to have a nature ramble," she said brightly. "So be sure to come in warm, sensible clothes — and your wellingtons, of course."

Gillian's heart sank. Trudging along muddy lanes in the cold, with no-one talking to her — it would be awful!

"I've got a sore head," Gillian lied, at breakfast next morning.

But Mum wasn't so easily deceived.

"You'll be going for a lovely walk in the fresh air today," she reminded Gillian. "If that doesn't cure your headache, nothing will." And she bundled Gillian up in her cosiest clothes and packed her off to school as usual.

Gillian's class was soon lined up in the school playground, two by two, and she was relieved to be paired with Charlie Briggs, a shy boy, mad on insects, who actually smiled at her.

Gillian trudged along with Charlie, her eyes on the ground. But soon she lifted her face as she saw that the sun had come out and it suddenly seemed less cold. The sky was a wonderful rain-washed blue. Then she gazed, fascinated, at a rainbow in a puddle . . .

As the gaily-clad little procession wound its way along, a bird began to chirp and, just in front of them, a squirrel ran down one tree and up another.

Gillian found herself looking around eagerly and listening with interest to Mrs Palmer.

"Now this is Wendover Farm —" the teacher's voice rang out clearly "— and Mr and Mrs Bellamy have given us permission to walk through. I hope you'll all behave very well, and keep to the path. In a few moments, you'll see something very nice indeed . . ."

What could it be, Gillian wondered, as they made their way along.

Then, rounding a bend, they all drew up, with little gasps of surprise and delight.

Below them, where the ground dipped a little to form a miniature valley, grew hundreds — no, thousands, maybe even millions — of beautiful white snowdrops. Tiny, gleaming, delicate flowers, their snowy petals veined with tender green, they hung their dainty heads, and fluttered gently in the grass. So little, so frail, so sweet, so brave . . .

"Oh, aren't they lovely?" Gillian cried, clasping her hands together, almost overcome with wonder. It was the prettiest sight she'd ever seen!

Soon Mrs Palmer was turning them round, to march them back to school.

"Come on, dreamer," she said to Gillian, but in such a nice, understanding way.

And then they were off again, straggling along muddy lanes in the pale sunlight, their snug duffel coats and anoraks making vivid patches of colour.

All the children were suddenly chatting and laughing together excitedly.

"I've got a rabbit called Benjamin," Rosemary Carter told Gillian, turning round unexpectedly.

"Have you?" Gillian was all interest. "I've got a kitten called Sparky."

All the other children began talking about their pets. And when Paul Halford slipped her a toffee — a liquorice one, it's true, the sort he didn't like much — Gillian felt so happy. What a wonderful day it had been! She couldn't wait to get home to tell Mum and Dad.

They weren't there when she got in. Dad wasn't due home from work yet, and Mum had gone to the hairdresser's. But Grandad was there, sitting hunched up at his desk, in a corner of the big dining-room.

Gillian, bursting in, all bright-eyed excitement, looked across at him thoughtfully.

Poor Grandad, he looked lonely somehow — and not at all grumpy or frightening.

"Hello, Grandad." She went over to him, giving him a hug.

He looked down at her and she gave a brilliant smile.

"Do you know, Grandad — I think I'm going to like the country, after all. I'm glad we've come to live here with you."

And then, though puzzled to see tears in his eyes, Gillian told Grandad about the snowdrops. ❏

Gentle Touch

THESE hands now aged without compare
From times when they were young and fair,
And full of strength that never shirked
The endless chores they daily worked!
Yet though they're wrinkled now, and frail,
Their gentle touch will never fail.
For, as they smooth a worried brow
With love and tenderness, as now,
Or soothe the tears from toddler's face,
These hands hold life's eternal grace.
— *Elizabeth Gozney.*

Heart of ~of~ Gold

M ARCH winds." Melanie sighed as rain lashed the windows, driven by a bitter easterly wind. "Oh, no! My washing!" She tried to put little Freddie in his pram, but no sooner had she put him down, than he began to cry bitterly, his little cheeks glowing red.

"Oh, don't cry, Freddie," she pleaded. "I won't be a minute . . . I must get the washing in."

But Freddie continued to howl, kicking his legs furiously and baring his red, painful gums.

Melanie's heart gave a sudden lurch.

"Oh, poor little mite," she soothed, picking him up again. "To heck with the washing. I'll just have to do it all again later."

Then she saw Tilly from next door, battling against the wind and rain to take the washing from the line and stuff it in the basket before the wind could carry it off.

"Oh, Tilly," Melanie said as she opened the door to let the poor, drenched little woman in. "You're soaked through!"

"I knew you'd be busy with the baby and wouldn't have time," Tilly said, brushing rain from her nose. "So I brought it in for you. I hope you don't mind . . ."

"Mind? Oh, Tilly, you're an angel!"

Melanie saw the pink of a blush glow beneath Tilly's wind-reddened cheeks.

"Well, I must fly now," Tilly said, and giggled as she hurried off down the path.

Tilly had a heart of gold, Melanie thought gratefully, and always seemed to wear a smile. Yet she had little to smile about.

Tilly's husband had died when her four boys were small and now her sons were grown up and gone.

by
Teresa Ashby

Illustration by John Hancock.

She'd spent her life savings setting her boys up and now they were hard-working men, leading busy lives with families of their own, Tilly hardly ever saw them.

"Tilly," Melanie called after her. "Would you like to take a bit of cake home with you? My mother left me some baking . . . You can't leave empty-handed . . ."

It was the wrong thing to say. Melanie knew it at once when she saw Tilly's back stiffen and her shoulders square up.

She didn't turn around.

"No, thank you, Melanie." And then she was gone.

Melanie bit her lip. Now she'd offended her and she hadn't meant to. She closed the door, shutting out the bad weather and carried little Freddie through to the lounge.

"Now, Freddie," she murmured softly. "I do want to help Tilly, but I just don't know how."

TWO doors down, Sylvia Shaw was struggling to get to the front door with the aid of her crutches. She'd broken her leg last winter and was making a very slow recovery.

She opened the door and found Tilly, wearing a smile, as ever, clutching a bundle of magazines to her chest.

Sylvia felt cheered at once.

"Thought you'd appreciate something to read," Tilly said.

"That's very sweet of you," Sylvia replied gratefully. "Won't you come in out of the rain?"

"No, I won't stop," Tilly replied cheerfully.

"Please," Sylvia entreated. "I could do with some company. It's ages until Mike gets home from work and I'm tearing my hair out with no-one to talk to."

"Well . . . just for a minute, then." Tilly stepped across the threshold.

"You're an angel, Tilly. These magazines will keep me busy for ages!"

"Shall I make you a cup of tea while I'm here?" Tilly offered, with a ready smile.

"No, I can manage —" Sylvia began, but Tilly was already in the kitchen, clattering cups and saucers and boiling the kettle.

"Will you have one, too, Tilly?"

"No, thank you."

"All right, if you won't have a cuppa with me, let me at least pay for the magazines."

"No, thank you, Sylvia!"

Tilly had taken umbrage.

Even though things were difficult, she was so proud, Sylvia thought later when Tilly had gone.

"If only there was some way of paying her back," Sylvia mused. "Some way of showing how much she's loved and cared for."

IT wasn't long before the sun was out and helping the brisk wind to dry the pavements.

Tilly walked, hand-in-hand, with two small children, down to the playpark. There she spent a happy hour pushing them on swings, watching them shoot down the slide and whizzing them round on the roundabout.

After an hour, breathless and laughing, Tilly walked them to the corner shop on the way home.

"I see you're looking after Ben's two little ones again, Tilly," Mrs Fisher remarked. "They're a handful for you."

"Not at all," Tilly replied. "I enjoy every minute."

She told Ben the same when she delivered them home.

"You're an angel, Tilly," he said. "I've managed to get all my ironing done in the hour they've been with you."

"I bought them a few sweets," Tilly admitted. "I hope that's all right . . ."

"Tilly, you shouldn't have," Ben began. "I mean, it's too much, you shouldn't go spending money on them . . ."

He broke off, but felt the need to do something to untighten Tilly's lips.

"What I meant to say . . ." he blustered on, praying for inspiration. "I mean, won't you let me pay you for having the kids?"

"No, thank you." Tilly drew herself up to her full five feet one inch.

Ben watched her hurry off down the path. She was always in a rush, always going somewhere and usually on an errand for someone else.

"Dear, proud Tilly," he murmured.

* * * *

Two streets away, old Mr Perry tried to press a few coins into Tilly's hand.

"I know things are hard for you, Tilly," he insisted. "I want you to take this as a small token of my appreciation."

"No, thank you, Mr Perry," Tilly replied stiffly.

"Eh?" Mr Perry cupped his hand to his ear. "Can't hear you."

"I said, no thank you, Mr Perry," she repeated loudly. "I don't want any money. It was only a little bit of washing . . ."

"Which I would have to cart all the way down to the launderette if it wasn't for you," Mr Perry put in.

"Your hearing problems seems to be coming and going today, Mr Perry." Tilly shot him a look.

He gave her a mischievous grin and closed her fingers around the coins.

"Take it towards washing powder and heating the water . . ."

Shaking her head, Tilly gave one of her brilliant smiles.

"There's really no need," she began, but he was pretending to be deaf again and fully occupied with straightening his curtains.

When she'd gone, he found the coins he'd given her standing in a neat little stack beside the clock on the sideboard.

"Oh, Tilly, Tilly, Tilly." He sighed. "What are we going to do with you?"

BACK home, Tilly sat in a chair and tugged a cardigan around her shoulders.

It was chilly this evening, but not cold enough to switch on the fire. She'd just dozed off when the phone rang, but she woke immediately, answering it brightly.

"Mum? Hello, it's John."

"John!" She felt her cheeks flush pink with pleasure. John, her youngest, called every week without fail.

"I've managed to snatch some time off," he went on. "What do you think of having a big family bash next week?"

"Next week?" Tilly gulped, her eyes straying to the tin on the mantelpiece where she kept her emergency fund.

"I'm going to get in touch with Doug, Steve and David to see if they can come with their families.

"Think of it, Mum! We haven't had a get-together like this for years!

"Only it's coming up for the Easter holidays," he went on eagerly. "There'll be no school and . . ."

"Wh . . . where were you thinking of . . . ?" Tilly whispered.

"At home, of course — your home," John answered cheerfully. "Where better? If David can come in his camper, and Steve can bring his tent, we'll manage. What do you say, Mum?"

"I . . . I think it's a wonderful idea," Tilly mumbled weakly.

As soon as she'd put down the phone, Tilly picked up her emergency tin and prised off the lid.

A lone fifty-pence piece rattled in the bottom. She'd raided it just last week when the gas bill had turned up. How on earth was she going to feed four hefty lads, their wives and all their children? And she was too proud to tell them that money was a bit tight at the moment . . .

* * * *

A couple of days later, she found herself chatting to Melanie over the garden fence.

"They're all coming." Tilly sighed. "My whole family. And they're planning to stay for a week."

"You don't sound very pleased," Melanie pointed out, puzzled.

"Oh, but I am!" Tilly cried. "I'm delighted."

It was the same when she popped in to visit Sylvia — and Ben. They were all so pleased for her.

It was only old Mr Perry who saw through her strained smile. "You must be wondering how on earth you're going to feed them all for a week," he remarked, hitting the nail on the head.

A Century of Change

Screen Test

T was a Scot, John Logie Baird, who invented TV, though times have changed since those first hazy black and white pictures. He launched his first television service on September 30, 1929 and marketed the first sets, Baird Televisors, at 26 guineas each.

Six years later, on November 2, 1936, the world's first high-definition television broadcasting service was opened from Alexandra Palace, London. At that point, there were only about 100 sets in the country!

Sales boomed just before the Queen's Coronation and many watched TV for the first time on that day. Since then, television has become part of our every-day lives.

Now we have colour and a choice of channels. There are nature programmes, dramas, news reviews, chat shows, sports events, soap operas . . . We all have our favourites. Life just wouldn't be the same without TV.

John Logie Baird switches on!

• • • • • • • • 1920 - 1929 • • • • • • • •

"They always bring stuff with them . . ." she protested. That was true, but it was never enough and Tilly liked to put on a good spread.

"You struggled to raise them on your own, Tilly," Mr Perry said kindly. "They never went without. If they knew the hardship —"

· "Hardship?" Tilly was stung.

"Yes, Tilly! I know you gave up a lot for your boys, and that you've not got a great deal in the bank." His voice was kind and suddenly she sank into an armchair, her face creased with despair.

"I don't want to burden them with my problems, Mr Perry," she whispered, at last.

"You're their mother, not a burden," Mr Perry tutted. "They'd be mortified if they knew how much their visits cost you."

Still Waters

WHEN the evening light is lying
  On the loch, with no birds flying,
Not a fin to fret the water,
  Not a breath of wind to scatter
Clouds held motionless and high
  In the arches of the sky.

Then, it seems, all beauty linge
  Where the light strokes lazy
    fingers
Over rolling braes and highlan
  Cottages and tree-clad island
Framed by spiky grasses browr
  In a world upside down.

Cool and clear, these pools of silence,
   Holding all the sunset's radiance,
Jewel-bright in the shining colours,
   Mountain crags and purple hollows
Caught a moment, held in space,
   Mirrored in the water's face.
                    — *Brenda G. Macrow.*

Lochan near Lochailort.

Dennis Hardley.

On the morning the boys were due to arrive, Tilly cleaned the house from top to bottom. She was just taking a well-earned coffee break when she heard a noise by the front door. Thinking one of the boys had arrived early, she rushed to the door.

But there was no-one there — just a box brimming with groceries!

"There's been a mistake," Tilly whispered, but there was no mistaking the note sticking out of the top.

To Tilly, it read. *With love and thanks.*

"I'll just find out who sent it and send it right back," Tilly said but, although she tried to sound cross, she found herself choking back a tear.

Half an hour later, she opened the door to shake out a duster and found four bulging carrier bags.

For Tilly, the note with them read. *Have a great time this week.*

And, an hour after that, another parcel appeared again with a note. This one read: *To our dear Tilly — what would we do without you?* Finally, she answered a knock on the door to find Mr Perry standing on the doorstep, holding a bottle of wine.

"Don't give me any of that 'can't possibly' rubbish," he said before Tilly could utter a word. "I bought it for you, so enjoy it and accept it with good grace, because I'm certainly not taking it back."

"Thank you, Mr Perry," Tilly replied steadily. "Thank you very, very much indeed."

"No-one knows better than you that it's better to give than receive." Mr Perry chuckled. "Perhaps now you'll understand that, and practise what you preach! You get so much pleasure from giving your time to others, be a real angel and let them give you something in return."

* * * *

Her son John arrived first, trooping in with a decorating table under his arm and a huge grin on his face.

"What's all this? I don't need any decorating . . ."

But John knew that wasn't the truth.

"Someone told you!" Tilly cried.

"Several someones," John admitted. "Do you realise how many people love and care about you, Mum? Why did you let us all go on assuming you were managing?"

He put the table down and gave her a hug.

"I'm where I am — what I am — because of you," he murmured. "I love you, Mum."

A few weeks ago, she'd have given him a swipe and told him off for being so soppy and sentimental. Now, to her dismay, Tilly burst into tears.

"You were always there for us when we needed you," John went on, holding her tight. "Now we want to be here for you . . . please let us."

And Tilly, her heart bubbling over with love and joy, could only nod her agreement. ❑

KATHY gazed at me across the breakfast table.

"Ple-ease, Mum. I'll absolutely die of shame if I don't have them. I'd be the only one without. And you wouldn't want that, would you?" she implored.

I doubted that *she'd* die of shame, but it was definitely on the cards that *I* might when the bank manager decided to send me a warning letter — which he could do any day now.

Growing Pains

— by Ceri Evans —

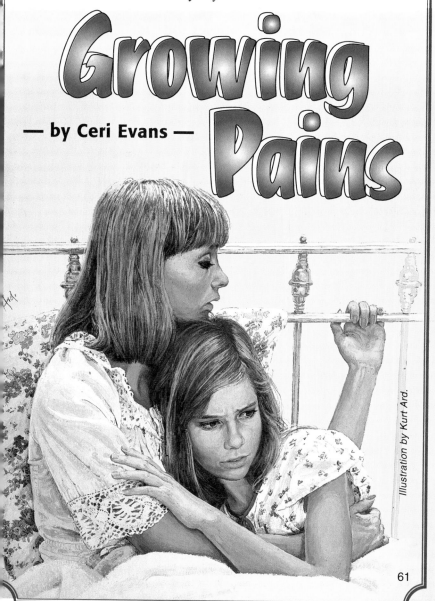

Illustration by Kurt Ard.

"I'm sorry, love. I really can't afford to buy designer trainers. Not this month anyway. Besides, they just aren't worth it when you're growing so fast. You would be out of them in weeks — long, long before you'd got the use —"

"I'd wear them every minute of the day. Honestly, Mum," Kathy promised.

"But they're not allowed at school."

"Well, every other minute," she conceded.

I SHOOK my head and pushed the toast towards her. She ignored it, which was most unusual as she was always ravenous. Evidently food had now come second place to fashion.

I guess that's what it's like at twelve these days. But I suppose it always was . . . You have to keep up with trends — fit in. I'd been no different in my day.

Kathy pouted at me.

"Everybody else's mother's buying them."

She ought to get a record made of that, I'd heard it so often before and I knew exactly what it meant. Some mother somewhere, with more cash than sense, had bought a fancy pair of trainers and set the ball rolling.

Other parents with a lower cracking point than mine had pushed their credit cards towards the meltdown limit and the rest of us, who were determined to hold out, were being held to ransom.

Except I don't give in to moral blackmail. Not often, anyway. I mean, the mountain bike for Christmas was different. She needed one. Well, sort of. And perhaps I *could* have got a cheaper model than the one she'd liked, but, as she'd said, the extra must have meant it was a better one; reliable and safe.

Anyway, I'd gone for broke on that and, given it was only February now, our finances hadn't had a chance to recover. Some days I wondered if they ever would. Not, probably, till Kathy had left home!

"I'm sorry," I said firmly, "but I just can't manage it. If you need trainers, you'll have to settle for whatever Dad and I can stretch to."

Kathy glared at me and, grabbing her schoolbag, headed for the door.

"You're just being mean! If only I could swap you for a decent family."

That really hurt. I watched her go with tears welling in my eyes. I mean, if Bob and I had had the money we'd have bought the earth for Kathy. We'd have spoilt her rotten.

When you've waited for so long and gone to the very edges of despair to have a child, there's nothing you wouldn't do for them . . . except go into debt.

If only I could swap you. Kathy's words went echoing around my head. I could remember saying much the same to my own mother once, although I'd no idea how it must have hurt her. Until now.

The memory was as fresh as yesterday.

I'd wanted jeans. I'd insisted they were Levis, which Mum couldn't possibly afford, despite the fact she did two part-time cleaning jobs. She'd taken me to the market and, confronted with a choice of several cheap and serviceable pairs in an unknown brand, I'd thrown a shameful tantrum.

I'd said she couldn't be my *real* mother — real mothers gave their daughters everything they wanted. It was only wicked substitutes who didn't. I bet I didn't really belong to them at all. I didn't even look like her or Dad!

It was so very silly that, by the time I'd wolfed down a burger and cola, I'd almost forgotten all about it. So I'd got a nasty shock when I'd found my red-eyed mother sitting sadly in her old armchair at home, an album in her lap and piles of used-up tissues by her side.

I really hadn't meant to hurt her and I'd felt so guilty.

She'd slid an arm around me and begun to turn the pages of the album. There were snapshots of her, blooming through the swelling stages of her pregnancy.

I'd not seen them before and wondered why.

"You have. You've just forgotten." Mum had shrugged philosophically. "We used to look at these a lot when you were very little . . . but then there comes a time when children are embarrassed by their baby photographs, so I put them by. These days I only look at them when I'm on my own."

I'd gazed in fascination at the bulging floral smock.

"It's me," I'd breathed in disbelief.

And there I was, each month a bump grown bigger until, at last, I lay, a wrinkled little red-faced newborn, in her arms.

"An hour old," she'd murmured wistfully.

"I was hideous! However could you love a thing like that?" I'd asked in amazement.

"So easily, so very easily . . ."

I'd suddenly recalled my tantrum in the market and blushed to realise that she could love me still, through my ugliest of moments and my cruellest of taunts.

I'd leaned my head against her shoulder and felt her stroke my hair forgivingly.

We'd looked at those photos quite often after that . . .

Of course, I couldn't do the same with Kathy, since I hadn't anything to show till she was five. All *I* could do was wait and pray her temper would have sweetened by the time she came home.

But maybe she was right. I knew that, having had to wait so long, I must be older than the average parent, so maybe I *was* mean as well. Out of touch. Perhaps I could re-organise this month's budget to allow

Take A Letter . . .

ANNE and I were sitting having a cup of tea when she started reminiscing.

"John, do you remember. . .?"

Thank goodness we are both blessed with good memories. This time we recalled the occasion Anne was in hospital in St Andrews — over 20 years ago now.

I was walking down Seagate in Kingsbarns on my way to get the advice of a retired shepherd when Mary, a neighbour, seeing me passing, came out of her cottage to enquire about Anne.

I told her how she was getting on and then Mary asked me to wait for a minute.

She rushed into her cottage and, after a moment or two, came out with an envelope. Would I give it to Anne? She might want to buy something from the hospital trolley . . .

I took the envelope in that evening and when Anne opened it, out fell a five-pound note — a lot of money in those days.

Anne shed a tear and I had to wipe my eyes. It was one of those kind gestures we will never forget. It was money poor Mary could barely afford.

I was instructed by Anne, as I left her bedside that evening, to bring her next day, without fail, notecards, pen and stamps. She's a great believer in saying thank you in written form, not by telephone.

Anne wanted to thank Mary for her most thoughtful and generous gift — but she also wanted to do something else . . .

THE highlight of the day in the ward was when Matron came round and asked each patient how she was and distributed the mail.

Every morning she'd stop and speak to the lady in the bed next to Anne.

The Farmer And His Wife

for those trainers . . .

"I'm sorry," Kathy mumbled as she flung her arms around me later that day.

"You ought to be in school," I said, bewildered.

"Lunchbreak."

Had the wretched morning really gone so fast? I could hardly believe it.

"I had to come and tell you I'm sorry, Mum. The rubbish I was talking about swapping you and Dad. I didn't mean it, honestly, I didn't. I reckon you could swap *me* for a better daughter, though."

She hiccuped through a sob, then silence hung between us for a moment, while I tried to swallow down the lump which blocked my throat.

"You wouldn't, would you?" Kathy added anxiously.

I hugged her close.

"We've always told you that we chose you specially," I comforted.

"Sorry, Agnes. There's not one for you today." There never was.

Anne felt really sorry for this lassie and had discovered she lived and worked on a farm at Balmullo with her widowed father.

Next night, Anne told me to sit and read a magazine whilst she wrote.

When she handed me one of the cards to post, I was surprised to see the address — St Andrews Cottage Hospital. That was where I was sitting at that moment!

Next day, while on her rounds, Matron stopped at Agnes' bed.

"Agnes, there's one for you."

Agnes grasped the letter in delight and read the carefully worded best wishes. Tears of happiness shone in her eyes.

"Mrs Taylor, it's from you!" With that, she jumped out of bed and put her arms around Anne and hugged her.

"It's the first letter I've ever got!" she cried. "Thank you."

As we chatted about the incident later, Anne quite rightly pointed out how lovely it is to receive a card or letter.

So get writing!

by John Taylor

"And nothing's changed."

It never will. I guess there'll always be one dreadful day in every mother's life when that enormous gulf between the generations yawns in front of her and the closest ties appear to be unravelling.

I've peered into that chasm now from both sides for myself, wanting not to be my mother's daughter till I saw she'd given birth to me. Wanting even more to be my daughter's mother though someone else gave birth to her.

But I've been lucky and my worlds have pulled themselves together again . . .

"Maybe we'll see if Dad can stump up for your trainers," I say quietly.

But Kathy shakes her head.

"They're not important, Mum. Not any more."

She's right. Yet maybe I will buy them for her now . . . ❏

JIM faced Maggie across the kitchen table, anger and pain clouding his eyes.

"And when, just when, do I come first? It's 'Beth needs me', or 'I promised Helen', or 'I've just got to help little Katie out'.

"I'm fed up with it. As far as I'm concerned, you might as well let them all come and live here! I don't seem to count at all . . ." He said a lot more besides before he stormed out, telling her finally that she needn't expect him back.

Maggie was stunned, her heart pounding in shock as she heard the front door slam shut.

She'd been standing making tea when Jim had lost his temper. Now she sat down heavily. What had she said to so upset him?

Yet, in her heart of hearts, she knew. With hindsight, she realised he'd been building up to this outburst for some time.

It had been ages since he'd done anything other than listen to her. He hadn't talked, not really talked, for months now.

She poured herself a cup of tea.

He'll be back, she told herself. They had a good marriage . . .

Maggie had been bowled over by Jim. He was such fun to be with, so easy going, so understanding. And he'd been totally undeterred when she'd told him about her three sisters.

"There are four of us altogether," she'd explained. "When Mum died, I was the oldest at twelve, and I promised her I'd look after them."

"What about your dad?"

A shadow had crossed her face.

"My dad just gave up when my mum died. Oh, he went to

Illustration by
M. Thorsen.

work each day, paid for things, but he left everything else to me." She'd seen by his face that he was put out and had jumped to her father's defence.

"You're not to think badly of him. He loved my mother dearly. He just found it difficult to manage without her. And, before he had the chance to come to terms with it, he had his first heart attack. There were two more after that, and he died when I was sixteen."

He'd gazed at her in admiration.

"And you brought your sisters up alone?"

She'd nodded.

"It wasn't so hard. They all helped out. Even little Katie knew how to keep her room clean. I just did my best.

"And now they're all grown-up." She'd smiled proudly.

Taken For Granted

by Anna Bradley

"Helen got married, then Beth went to college, and little Katie has gone into nursing. They all live their own lives now."

He'd taken her into his arms and cuddled her.

"And now I'm going to take care of you."

And he had. At first she'd been rapturously happy in her own house. Jim was so strong and dependable, he'd taken charge of everything.

But things didn't work out as they'd hoped. They weren't blessed with the baby they'd both longed for — and Maggie's sisters began to take up more and more of her time. They

67

still expected her to be there for them, any time, any place.

When Helen had her twins, and then a third baby soon after, she needed a lot of help and Jim hadn't minded at first. Now, when Maggie was expected to baby-sit at a moment's notice, he didn't say anything but he did look disappointed.

THEN Beth, who'd sailed through university and landed a good job, had a series of very unfortunate relationships.

All her romances followed the same pattern — forget big sister when the relationship is flourishing but demand help, even at three in the morning, when things go wrong.

Katie wasn't married, didn't require a baby-sitter and had no men troubles. She was hoping one day to marry the trainee doctor she'd been dating for the past year.

Katie's trouble was that she went through money like it was going out of fashion. Maggie had helped her out several times. Twice she had settled all her credit cards and now she needed help because her car was about to be repossessed.

This time Jim had put his foot down.

"No more. Did you hear me? They're all just taking advantage of you."

The words rang in her ears as she let herself out of the house and hurried along the road to catch the bus to work.

She enjoyed her job at the local estate agent's, though it was nothing glamorous. Just putting details in envelopes for posting, making the tea for customers and staff, filing away the sheets left out by the salesmen and generally making herself useful.

But today she couldn't settle — she couldn't help worrying about her relationship with Jim. She loved him dearly, he was the most important person in her life . . . The last thing she wanted was to lose him.

"Do you mind if I pop out to the chemist's? I've a real headache and I don't have anything for it," she asked her boss mid-morning.

Mr Hardcastle tut-tutted sympathetically. Maggie was the most

Skye Dreams

WHEN wearied by the daily rou
With little time to take our ea
A swift solution may be found
For those who love the Hebrides -
We only have to close our eyes
To see the hills of Skye arise!

The Cuillin catching wisps of cloud,
The Red Hills with their granite
scree,
And Blaven's furrowed ridges prouc
Towering above the restless sea,
Where sunlight on Loch Slapin play
And cries of seabirds haunt our da

Dream isle whose silhouette inspire
The artist's brush, the poet's pen,
When city life the spirit tires,
It brings us comfort, now and then
To see you looming through the rai
And feel our hearts grow young
again!

— *Brenda G. Mac*

Blaven, Skye.

Willie Shand.

reliable of his staff.

"Of course — walk round the shops a bit, give yourself some space. Take the day off. Chill out." He was rather proud of his modern vocabulary, learned from his fifteen-year-old daughter.

Maggie smiled weakly.

Once out, she felt much better. And, as she walked, she suddenly had an idea. She hurried along, overtaking small chattering groups as she made her way to Merton's toy shop. She looked in the window for several minutes before plucking up courage to go inside.

"A complete railway, Madam? How old is your son?" Mr Merton smiled at her.

Maggie looked back, unflinching.

"It's not for my son — it's for my husband. He's always — er — wanted . . ."

"No need to explain." Mr Merton looked very happy. "Many of our customers are grown-up!"

Maggie soon found just what she was looking for — at the right price. She used most of the money she'd meant to give to Katie.

Back at the office, Mr Hardcastle was selling a semi to a young couple and she put the parcel at the back of her desk. All she wanted now was for it to be five o'clock.

In a slack moment, she ordered a taxi.

Today she wanted to arrive home on time. Today she wanted to be home before Jim. Too often lately he had been first home. She didn't dare let herself think that he might not be there . . .

S HE was startled to see the lights on upstairs when the taxi pulled up. Had he come home early to pack? She hurried up the drive. "Jim? Jim?" She started upstairs, but he met her half-way.

"Are you all right?" He looked anxious. "I rang Mr Hardcastle and he said you weren't well." There was no mention of the morning, just deep concern on his face.

"Yes — it was just a headache." She smiled and then kissed him. "Oh, Jim, I felt awful, I . . ."

He put his fingers on her lips.

"Don't say any more. It was my fault. I was jealous.

"Of course, you must look after your sisters. They've thought of you as their mother for years. You can't stop now. I understand."

"No, Jim." She pulled herself out of his arms and sat down on the stairs.

"You were right. If I was a real mother, I'd have let them go. I can see that now. While I run round after them, they'll never be independent.

"I'll offer to go with Katie to see the bank manager. She can get a proper loan and learn to manage her money. I'll not let Beth take me for granted. And Helen will have to learn to organise herself, no more instant baby-sitting, unless it's a real emergency."

"Sh." He put his fingers on her lips again and led her into the dining-room where a large square parcel dominated the table. "I just wanted to say sorry."

Speechless, she handed over her parcel.

"And I got this for you."

He started to open it, while she ripped the paper off her box. It was a doll's-house — a real doll's-house with lights.

"I didn't get any furniture. I thought you might like to collect it yourself bit by bit. It could become a hobby."

She turned to him, tears streaming down her face.

"How did you know? How did you know I wanted one?"

"How did I know that you longed for your own daughter so that you could play with a doll's-house? It was easy." He smiled. "It was probably the same way you knew I wanted a son so I could play with his train set!"

They went into each other's arms.

After a moment, she pulled away. This seemed a good time to tell him her other news.

"I had the results from the clinic this morning. They said there's no

Hooray For Hollywood!

FORGET it, Louis. No Civil War picture ever made a nickel." This was Irving Thalberg's advice to Louis B. Mayer when he first suggested making "Gone With the Wind", the film which was to become the biggest box-office success of its day, going on to earn millions. Made in 1939, the film has become a Hollywood classic.

In the same year, no fewer than 387 other films were released. They included "The Wizard of Oz", starring Judy Garland, "Stagecoach" — the film which made a star of John Wayne — and "Ninotchka" in which the inscrutable Garbo actually laughed. Small wonder that the average American family spent 25 dollars that year on cinema tickets — an all-time record.

But it was "Gone With The Wind" which dwarfed all the rest, starring an unknown Vivien Leigh as Scarlett O'Hara and Clark Gable as Rhett Butler, a role for which Errol Flynn had originally been considered. The film won nine Academy Awards and gave us one of cinema's most famous lines: "Frankly, my dear, I don't give a damn."

• • • • • • • • 1930-1939 • • • • • • • •

reason why we can't have children but they will offer us treatment if we haven't succeeded by next year."

Again, he held her close.

"Don't worry. It'll be the icing on the cake if a baby comes, but if it doesn't happen, then I'll still be happy. I'm married to the most marvellous woman in the world."

And her heart was full as he reached out for her.

The phone rang downstairs, but she ignored it and reached up to kiss him again. ❑

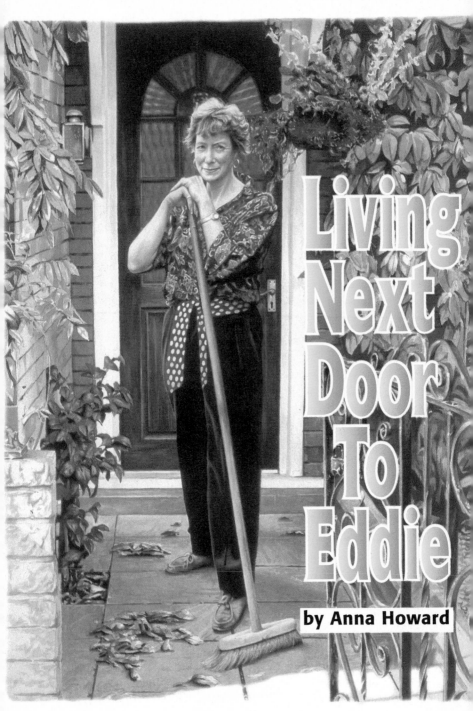

Living Next Door To Eddie

by Anna Howard

W HAT do you think, lass?" Charles Gregg put an arm around his wife's shoulders.

Daphne leaned against him and gazed around the workshop of their new home. Always neat, Charles had arranged his tools above the bench and the drawing desk stood in the corner with his comfortable swivel chair in front of it.

"I think it looks like your dream, Charlie love," she said. "Just as you wanted it. You could weave magic in here."

Hanging from the ceiling were kites of every shape, size and colour. After he was offered early retirement from his job as a draughtsman, he'd turned to his beloved hobby of designing kites.

Daphne wanted to live near the sea and they'd found this house, in a perfect setting, and with plenty of space.

They'd more or less settled in and the workshop was the last room to be arranged.

"Just a few more pieces of equipment to unpack," Charles said, releasing Daphne and heading for the jumble of boxes on the floor, "then I can get on. Who'd have thought I'd get firm orders after all this time?" He chuckled happily.

"I'm going to have another look around the garden," Daphne told him. "I'll try to make a list of what we need next season."

She left Charles to his unpacking and wandered outside. From the corner of her eye, she caught rhythmic glimpses of the small boy next door as his swing carried him higher than the hedge.

His mother had called round the day they'd moved in, introducing herself as Fiona. The boy hadn't come, too, but had climbed on to his garden gate and stayed there, scowling and pushing it to and fro.

Daphne hadn't seen them since and was disappointed they hadn't become more friendly.

She prowled the garden, pulling up a weed here and there. At the end of the hedge dividing the two properties, there was a gap. It was overgrown, but wide enough for someone to pass through.

The creaking of the swing had stopped and, on impulse, Daphne popped her head round the gap.

The boy was standing, prodding the grass with a stick. The untidy red hair falling on to his forehead reminded Daphne of her own son at that age.

"Hello." She smiled at him. "How are you today? Did you enjoy your swing?"

He stared at her for a moment and the resemblance tore at her heart. It could almost have been Andrew standing there.

"Go away!" he shouted suddenly. "You're not my gramma and you shouldn't be in that house."

He glared at her before running away down the garden.

Fiona James was watching her son from the back door and saw him run behind the holly bush.

"Come in now, Eddie," she called. "Daddy will be home soon."

Slowly, the child emerged, scuffing his shoes along the path, a dishevelled, grubby elf. He pushed past his mother into the kitchen.

"They're still there," he said. "They're doing things in the garden."

"Yes." Fiona nodded severely. "And you were very rude.

"I know you miss Gramma, but it isn't that lady's fault. We don't own that house." She closed the back door decisively.

Daphne was still standing by the hedge, shocked by the boy's outburst, when she felt a hand on her shoulder. She turned to find her husband looking at her anxiously.

"I don't think we're too welcome next door," she said unsteadily, pushing her face into his chest.

"Give it time," Charles soothed. "We've only been here a couple of weeks. Wait for the boy to come to *you*.

"Now, how about some tea?"

NEXT day, Daphne decided to have a baking session, as she often did when she had something on her mind. She found it soothing, rolling out pastry and mixing ingredients together. By the afternoon, she'd made up her mind to call on Fiona, taking round a fruit pie.

Resisting the temptation to use the gap in the hedge, Daphne went through the front gate, carefully carrying a cherry pie, and rang her neighbour's doorbell.

It was a few moments before there was any response, then the door opened.

"Oh!" said a flustered Fiona in surprise.

"Hello. I've baked far more than we can eat and our freezer's full up," Daphne greeted her. "Do you all like cherry pie?"

"Yes, how kind." Fiona smiled. "Eddie and I are in the kitchen. Please come in. I've just put the kettle on."

They went into the bright, comfortable kitchen where Eddie was working at a colouring book on the table.

"Hello, Eddie," Daphne said. "I've brought you a pie."

He threw her a hostile glance, scrambled down, and ran out of the room.

"Eddie!" Fiona scolded but he didn't come back.

"Oh, dear." She sighed. "I'm sorry he's so rude."

She busied herself making tea.

"My parents used to live in your house and Eddie seems to feel you shouldn't be here." She turned to look apologetically at her visitor.

"Mum and Dad decided to move to Florida when his arthritis got worse. There will be long visits, of course, but it's not the same."

"I know the feeling," Daphne sympathised, sipping her tea.

"My son and his wife have just emigrated to Australia. He was offered a wonderful job, and I'm glad for him, but I don't suppose I'll have the chance to get really close to my grandchildren. If they have any," she added wistfully, with a small sigh.

"Eddie adores his grandmother. He misses her terribly. So do I," Fiona revealed.

They chatted comfortably together for a while.

"I wonder — does Eddie like kites?" Daphne asked suddenly.

"Well, I don't know — he's never had one before." Fiona sounded surprised.

"My husband designs and makes them," Daphne said, not without pride. She heard a slight sound from the passage and nodded her head towards the door.

Fiona smiled back with perfect understanding.

"I wonder if Eddie would like to come and see a new kite being tested tomorrow in the garden," Daphne went on, raising her voice a little. "About two o'clock, if it isn't raining."

She went home with a spring in her step. She and Charles had always done everything as a team and winning over new neighbours would be no exception.

Next afternoon, a yellow shape took to the air, flying high above the hedge.

Soon, Charles heard a rustling on the other side. He reeled the kite in and put his head through the gap.

"Come and have a look, Eddie," he called. "You're just in time to give me some help."

Hesitantly, the boy approached as Charles laid the kite on the lawn.

"Would you hold it up for me, as high as you can, please?" he said. "We'll soon have it off the ground again."

With an expert pull and flick of the string, the kite was airborne.

"It's a great big bird," Eddie said, his head tilted right back to watch.

"It's an eagle," Charles explained. "I made it in memory of an eagle called Goldie, that escaped from the zoo."

He handed the string to Eddie.

"You hold her for a minute."

Daphne appeared from the kitchen.

"How's it going?" she asked.

"Come and give us a hand," Charles said. "It's flying well today."

Just then, a gust of wind almost hauled the boy off his feet.

Daphne stepped behind him and caught the string, taking the strain.

Unconsciously, Eddie leaned back against her legs, fitting his small body naturally into hers.

"Sometimes, if the wind is strong, it takes two or even three people to keep a kite steady," Daphne said.

After a while, the breeze calmed and she passed the string to Charles.

"You've got an excellent helper here," she told him, smiling at Eddie. "I'll just go and get some juice now." And she went off to the kitchen.

Daphne had been baking again, this time with another motive. Putting some cakes on a tray, she added a jug of lemonade and carried it outside.

"What have we got here?" Charles asked as she set the tray down on the garden table.

"They're called chocolate brownies and they're an American cake," she explained.

"Try one, Eddie, and see if you like it. They make a lot of them in Florida and I expect you'll have them when you visit your grandma."

Eddie demolished a cake in silence.

"Nice," he said finally. "I might be going there soon."

"I daresay you will." Charles smiled. "But, meanwhile, how would you like to come and help me fly the kite on the beach on Saturday? It's better where there are no trees."

"Oh, yes please!" Eddie said, beaming.

"I think we'd better ask your mother first," Daphne cautioned. "We'll take her some brownies to taste, shall we?"

Daphne picked up the plate and, as they went through the gap in the hedge, a small hand crept into hers.

Fiona was on the terrace, scrubbing at something. She looked round at Daphne's approach and smiled.

"Have you had a good time?" she asked.

"Mummy, these cakes are American and there's a lovely yellow kite called Goldie and can I go to the beach Saturday and —"

"Hold on!" Fiona interrupted, laughing. "One thing at a time. Go and get washed first."

"It worked then," she said to Daphne, as Eddie scampered indoors.

"Fingers crossed, but I think so." Daphne grinned.

Fiona bent down to gather up her bucket and sponge, revealing the baby's highchair she'd been cleaning. As she straightened up, her loose sweater clung to her body briefly and she put a hand to her back in a familiar gesture.

Daphne smiled to herself. It looked like it wouldn't be too long before she could offer her services as a baby-sitter . . .

Suddenly she was sure she was going to like living next door to Eddie! ❏

Craigievar Castle, Aberdeenshire

COMPLETED in 1626 by Aberdeen merchant Willliam Forbes, Craigievar is a fairytale castle in a lovely setting. Turrets and balustrades decorate the soft pinky exterior and, inside the castle, the rooms are a delight to explore. Extravagant moulded ceilings are a feature of the beautifully decorated rooms and there's a wealth of fascinating period furniture.

CRAIGIEVAR CASTLE, ABERDEENSHIRE : J CAMPBELL KERR

Illustration by Jim Dewar.

I'M not going!" I cried. "You'll all have to go without me."

"Not going?" Mum gasped. "But you have to go. It's *your* party . . ."

"I can't," I insisted. "I look awful and it's too late to do anything about it."

"But, Carrie . . ." Mum's face fell.

"I'm sorry, Mum. You'll just have to tell everyone I'm ill, or something . . ."

I couldn't bear to see the disappointment on her face a moment longer. She'd put so much into this party and had spent ages making sure everything was just right.

I knew I was letting her down, but what else could I do?

"How can I let Matt see me like this?"

I turned and rushed up to my room.

It was Gran who'd started it all.

"Your problem," she'd said, "is your hair. Look at it!"

"My hair?" I'd peered in the mirror and given my long golden tresses a casual flick. I'd been growing it for years and had just about got it the way I wanted.

"What's wrong with it?"

"What's right with it!" Gran had sniffed. "You're just like the girls in those Australian soaps. Why don't you have it cut properly . . .? Or at least have a perm!"

"I thought it looked . . ." I'd begun, but hadn't bothered to finish. What was the point?

"If you ask me," Grandad had said, "it's not your hair that's the problem. Your hair's lovely."

Good old Grandad. Trust him to come up trumps and stick up for me.

"No," he'd gone on, "the problem is your clothes."

"My *clothes*?"

COMING OF AGE

"That dress . . ." Grandad had continued knowledgeably. "All that lilac and lime green — it's a bit, well, violent. If you ask me, you can't beat good old navy blue and white . . ."

No use telling Grandad that good old navy blue and white were hardly the height of Nineties fashion.

Dad had put his paper down and come to my rescue.

"Leave the lass alone!" he'd countered. "Her hair's gorgeous, her clothes are great. If it wasn't for all that muck plastered over her face, she'd be perfect!"

"Her face is fine," Gran had chipped in. "Or it would be if she did something with that big lock of hair in her eyes . . ."

AUNTIE Jean had come in then. She'd been a bit of a rebel herself in her day and I often heard Gran moaning at her still about the way she dressed. She'd stand up for me!

"You look fantastic!" Auntie Jean had said. "All ready for the party? Your mum's just putting the finishing touches to the cake.

"What's up? This is your birthday. Twenty-one today!" She'd looked closer and frowned. "You're supposed to be all bright and sparkling and you look as if someone just put your lights out."

They had done. I didn't say it, but I didn't have to. Auntie Jean had looked around, put her hands on her hips and begun to nod like someone who knows everything.

"Oh, I see," she'd said. "The crush-your-confidence brigade have been on at you, have they? You don't want to pay any heed to these old wrinklies!"

"I didn't say anything." Gran had sniffed. "I merely said that her hair . . ."

"Her hair's great!" Auntie Jean had said.

"And I tell you it's not her hair, it's her clothes," Grandad had muttered.

"Terrific dress!" Auntie Jean gave me a thumbs-up. "Fab colours."

"Make-up," Dad had muttered. "Far too much of it!"

"Nothing wrong with gilding the lily, John. Take no notice of them, Carrie. They're suffering from the 'our little girl is twenty-one and we're all feeling our age' syndrome."

"Thanks," I'd murmured, but even with Auntie Jean's kind words, my ego still felt badly dented. "But you don't have to be nice to me just because it's my birthday."

"I'm not . . ." Auntie Jean had begun to speak, but I'd already left the room.

I'd bumped into Mum in the hall.

"Carrie, what's wrong?"

That's when I'd told her I wasn't going to the party . . .

Up in my room, I sat in front of my mirror, staring at my reflection.

My hair didn't look that bad. Did it?

I'd been so pleased with it this afternoon. For once, it had gone just how I wanted it, but now I wondered if I was just fooling myself.

And was this green too strong? I was so delighted with the way it shimmered and I thought it brought out the green in my eyes. But maybe I was wrong.

What about my make-up? I'd spent ages this afternoon putting it on, copying the look from one of my magazines.

"No chance of ever getting big-headed in this family," Mum said, peeping round the door. "Can I come in?"

I nodded and she came into my room and sat down on my bed beside me.

"The others have gone on ahead to the hall. I just hope the cake's safe . . . you know what your dad's driving is like!"

I laughed.

"Although there wasn't much point sending the cake if you aren't going to be there."

I lowered my eyes, my laughter fading quickly.

I'M sorry, Mum," I whispered. "I know I've let everyone down, but I can't go out looking like this, I just can't!"

"Looking like *what*?" Mum cried. "Carrie, you look lovely."

"Mum," I said. "Does my hair look a mess? You would tell me, wouldn't you?"

"Your hair's beautiful," Mum said, tears glistening in her eyes. "Jean told me that Grandad didn't like your dress."

"He said it was violent."

"It probably reminds him of the Seventies, when Jean and I were your age." Mum laughed. "He hated all those psychedelic colours — said they gave him a migraine. He's just an old fuddy-duddy."

"And Dad says I've overdone my make-up."

"That's easy to explain. You're still his little girl. Today you look like a beautiful young woman and it makes him feel old and a little sad."

"But . . ."

How could I put my real fear into words without sounding silly?

"But . . ?"

"Mum, if Gran and Grandad and Dad can find so many faults, what if . . ?"

"Oh, love." Mum sighed. "You mustn't let them upset you. They didn't mean to, it's just . . . Well, they were trying to put right the things the others had said and they all ended up insulting you!"

"Horrible lot," I muttered.

"No, not at all." Mum smiled. "Like it or not, you're the best thing that's ever happened to any of them. They weren't deliberately trying to hurt you. It's because they love you so much that they feel they can speak their minds. But it's their minds, not anyone else's!"

"There is that." I laughed, feeling a little better. But not much.

"So you'll come to your party?"

"As long as I can wear a paper bag over my head!"

"That's my girl," Mum laughed, then hugged me.

There was still Matt. What if he didn't like my hair, or my dress, or my make-up? Or perhaps he'd hate something different, like my perfume or my shoes or my nail varnish.

"Wow!" he whispered softly when I walked into the hall.

I waited, holding my breath while he looked at me.

"You look . . . gorgeous," he breathed.

"My hair?" I fussed. "Should I have it cut? What about this dress? Is the colour right? Should I go home and change? And do you think I've got too much make-up on?"

He laughed and pulled me into his arms.

"You're perfect as you are," he said. "You can't improve on perfection."

I waited for the punch-line but it never came. Matt took me in his arms for the first dance and all my fears were swept away.

I daresay they could find fault with Matt, too. Gran wouldn't like the way he wore his hair and Dad wouldn't approve of the earring he wore. Grandad definitely wouldn't go for his bright orange shirt.

But I did . . . and, in the end, wasn't that all that mattered? ❏

ONCE, this land was frozen fast
 Under ice and Arctic wind.
When the glaciers thawed at last,
 What a scene they left behind!

Fold on fold of clouded hills
 Scarred with hanging corries steep
Crags where amber water spills
 Into lochs remote and deep.

Loch Morlich and the Cairngorms.

Gordon Henderson.

arm of the Cairngorms

 the glens, great forests rise,
  Red deer haunt the upland ways,
 agles circle on the skies,
  Sunlight on the river plays.

 hadows patch the hills with blue,
  Heather tosses in the breeze,
 rystal gems of every hue
  Shine amid the tumbled screes.

Hills ground down by glacial time,
  Still your charm our spirit cheers —
Wooded glens and heights sublime
  Call us back across the years.

— *Brenda G. Macrow.*

83

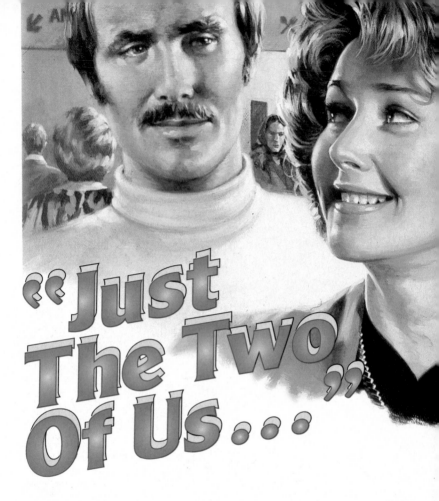

"Just The Two Of Us..."

THE airport lounge was filled with people drinking, eating, talking excitedly, or checking the departure monitors. Rachel put down her coffee cup and smiled across the lounge at Keith, who was wandering around the airport shops. But her gaze was soon drawn, once more, to a mother reading a story to her sleepy youngster.

It was something Rachel remembered doing when her children were young and she gave a small sigh.

A young man was walking the floor with his fractious youngster and trying not to look pained. It was a look she'd often seen on Keith's face, Rachel recalled wistfully.

She suddenly wondered how her children were coping at home without her. She hadn't wanted to leave them behind. She'd wanted them all to be together for a family holiday. But Clare, at eighteen, was going to Spain with her friends and Robbie, a year younger, was

by Alexandra Blue.

Illustration by Barcilon.

planning a camping expedition with his mates. There was *no way* either of them wanted to go to Menorca with their parents.

"You'll have a great time without us," Clare had said, helping them carry their luggage to the car. "You can eat paella to your heart's desire and play bingo with the other old people," she'd joked.

I should be cock-a-hoop — thrilled with this new-found freedom, Rachel thought. This holiday had cost a fraction of previous ones. Their luggage was minimal. And they had been able to choose a nice, quiet hotel rather than the usual large apartment complex with lots of sport and entertainment for the children.

So why was she feeling so depressed?

Rachel became aware that the little boy sitting next to her was studying the label on her hand luggage. With his blond hair and blue eyes, he wasn't unlike Robbie at the same age.

"Are you going on holiday?" she asked.

He nodded importantly.

"I'm going to Majorca on a big plane."

"Me, too," said his sister, sliding from her mother's knee. "We're staying in a pat hotel in Magawoof."

"An aparthotel in Magaluf," corrected their mother, smiling at Rachel. "This is our first family holiday abroad," she explained. "The kids are *so* excited they've been driving me mad. And my husband worked right up to the last minute so I had to do all the organising myself. I think I've packed everything but the kitchen sink."

Rachel laughed.

"I remember the feeling. It gets worse when they're teenagers. My kids used to pack their entire wardrobe."

"And never wear it?" guessed the young woman.

"Exactly!"

They smiled at each other and then both glanced towards their husbands.

Rachel noticed that Keith had moved round to the display of chocolates. The young woman's husband was still pacing the floor with their youngest.

WE booked this holiday last year, after the baby was born," the young woman revealed. "But I'm not so sure it was a good idea. She hasn't stopped crying since we left the house!"

"She'll settle," Rachel soothed. "May in Majorca is lovely — not too hot. And the children will have such fun in the swimming pool."

"I can swim," the little boy chipped in.

"I've got a rubber ring," said his sister proudly. "And a bikini."

Rachel laughed. She could remember Clare at the same age, strutting around in a magenta bikini. It had been lovely to watch the youngsters jumping fearlessly into the water . . .

But this year would be different . . . the family holiday a thing of the past.

"Where are you flying to?" the young mother asked.

"Menorca," Rachel said. "My husband booked it. It's supposed to be quieter than Majorca."

"That'll be nice. It must be awful having to put up with kids screaming and splashing water all over the place."

"I don't mind," Rachel admitted quietly and began to wonder again if she should have insisted that Clare and Robbie join them. They might look grown up, but they were still just teenagers.

The flight to Majorca was called. Rachel said goodbye to the young family and watched the little boy run down the corridor with his sister in hot pursuit. She could remember her own children bursting with excitement, carrying their snorkels and magazines, desperate to get the flight over with so they could dive into the pool . . .

Why did they have to grow up, Rachel thought sadly, suddenly fighting back a tear. I'm only forty. I'm too young to have outgrown the family holiday. I'm too young to spend my evenings playing bingo . . .

And then she saw them — a sister and brother, wandering sulkily after their parents. Wearing expressions of boredom and disdain, it was obvious they would rather be anywhere than joining their parents on the family holiday to the sun.

Rachel put a hand to her mouth to cover her smile. Who was she

ONE of the most sweeping reforms ever introduced by a British government was the establishment of the National Health Service. It was introduced by Aneurin Bevan, Health Minister in the post-war Labour Government, on July 5, 1948.

Britain's NHS promised to offer free medical treatment for the entire population. Dental care was included, as was the provision of free glasses and even wigs under prescription. 2,751 hospitals came under the control of the new regional health boards and local health authorities had responsibility for maternity and child welfare (with free orange juice for babies), health visiting, home nursing and clinical and ambulance services.

Before 1948, patients had fallen into two groups. Weekly wage earners, who were compulsorily insured, were on a doctor's "panel" and were given free medical attention (for which the doctor was paid quarterly by the government).

Most of the remainder paid the doctor a fee for his services at the time of illness.

The NHS promised an end to the worry of doctors' bills.

Aneurin Bevan

•••• 1940–1949 ••••

trying to kid? Last year's holiday had been a nightmare from start to finish. Clare had phoned home constantly to check up on her boyfriend. Robbie had suffered sunstroke.

There had been battles at mealtimes because they'd refused to eat anything other than burgers and chips. And it had been a struggle each morning to drag them out of bed.

"I thought this might cheer you up." Keith appeared by her side with a bag of goodies and slipped an arm around her. Inside the bag were all the necessities for a romantic week in Menorca — good wine, luxury chocolates and her favourite perfume.

"I've cheered up already," she said, kissing his cheek. "Our family holidays were lovely, but I'm really looking forward to there just being the two of us."

Keith smiled contentedly.

"A week of paella and bingo . . . Who could ask for more?" ❏

AT A STRETCH

by Olwen Richards

D AD was a bank clerk, but his true vocation lay elsewhere. He was a born collector. Not stamps or beer mats or antiques, like other fathers. No, mine had an affinity for something all *his* friends thought much more inexplicable if not bizarre, and all *my* friends considered much more interesting.

His speciality was what Mum called "lame dogs", which, in the early days, they were, quite literally.

We had a big, old house right on the outskirts of the town. It wasn't posh inside, so not even Mum was bothered by a trail of dirty pawmarks through the kitchen, or one more scrape off the paintwork. We were all too busy living each day as it came, and pets were part of that.

My parents believed that having animals would help us learn responsibility. Which, I suppose, it did, because we fed and watered, walked and bathed them, and never noticed being educated because it was such fun.

The house wasn't any posher outside, either. The garden romped and rambled in its own sweet way. It was paradise for us four boys, and a perfect haven for the waifs and strays Dad accumulated.

Not that he *meant* to start a mini zoo when he acquired Bram and Buster. He'd promised us a puppy. Nothing fancy, just a pot-luck mongrel from a litter down the road.

Mum had done her homework every bit as thoroughly as if we had our sights on Crufts. She'd read the books and sent him out with strict instructions not to buy the runt — she knew Dad was softer centred than a chocolate cream.

She just got one thing

Illustrations by Graham Williams.

wrong. She didn't go with him.

"You should be on a lead yourself," she muttered ruefully, when he arrived home with not just one, but two, puny, runny-nosed wee dogs.

"They're wretched looking, George. And how are we supposed to feed the extra one?"

"They're very cute." Dad smiled, a trifle sheepishly. "And Mr Bates says they'd pine if they were separated. I'm sure you'll make things stretch."

Mum did. She stretched the money round the vet's bill, then round each week's food, so neatly that we never noticed.

But that was only the beginning. Mr Bates had spread the word that we were a set of softies. All too soon, our house turned into a dumping ground for other people's animals.

We had them all. From poor unfortunates dumped anonymously over our back gate, to injured fox cubs; from scrawny chickens past their lay-by date to mangy rabbits, Dad never turned a single one away.

He'd simply look at Mum.

"Until we find a proper home . . ." he'd say, and she would tut reproachfully and go on stretching things. And finding homes.

Dad's compassion wasn't limited to fur and feather. It was an all-encompassing humanity which soon began collecting other kinds of lame dogs.

The first of those was Alf.

Coming home from work one dusky autumn afternoon, Dad discovered Alf asleep beneath the oak tree in the farthest corner of the garden. He had a few days' growth of stubble on his chin, a fair amount of soil about his person, a voice like gravel and a total fascination for us kids.

We'd never seen somebody pack his life into a canvas bag and tie it up with string.

As always, Dad persuaded Mum.

Alf, duly washed and kitted out in Dad's old clothes, was found a cosy corner in our garden shed. Although she didn't show it, Mum was, I think, relieved when Alf evinced a deep aversion to the idea of sleeping inside a house!

Besides, she had enough to cope with — stretching things again. A human mouth took more feeding than a few small animals.

Alf stayed the best part of a month, enthralling us with stories of adventures on the open road. Even Mum was sorry in a way to see him go.

But he had marked our house with one of those peculiar signs known only to the world of wanderers, and we were never afterwards without a temporary guest.

Yes, life in our house was nothing if not colourful. Then came the devastating news that we were being bought compulsorily to make way for road improvements.

Dad was furious, and so was everybody else. For months we entertained an army of protesters in our garden.

Dad took to making speeches, while Mum went quietly about the task of stretching even further, to provide an endless river of hot drinks.

Alf and all his travelling companions miraculously appeared simultaneously, pitching camp around us in a gesture of solidarity.

"Touching," Mum said softly. "I hadn't realised how much we were appreciated."

It didn't touch the council, though. They went ahead regardless and we moved into a semi in a faceless suburb. It had no soul, but, worse, it had no garden worth the name.

Our displaced persons were displaced again, and we were forced to find homes for almost all our animals.

We kept Bram and Buster and, no doubt, we were considerably better off. We just felt much poorer . . .

RIGHT, class, homework. Three pages, please, on 'What I did at Christmas'. And tidy, please."

We groaned in unison. I'd had to change schools when we moved and, while Miss Lacey was quite decent in her way, I wouldn't have admitted it for anything!

"She's nice," Mum said.

"Old prune-face," I said underneath my breath, remembering the essay which was guaranteed to put a damper on my holiday.

"Tim!" Mum chided.

"She is," I said sullenly. Although Miss Lacey didn't really have that many wrinkles. Just a few around her eyes and mouth . . .

"I reckon she was pretty," Mum said to Dad while we were having supper. She thought I was too busy making gravy moats around my mashed potato fortress to be bothered listening. Which I wasn't.

I'd discovered you could learn a lot of things you shouldn't if you lulled your parents into a false sense of security. I was paying great attention to conversations just then, in case they might let slip where they'd hidden the Christmas presents.

Dad shrugged.

"Difficult to tell," he said. "I don't suppose she's much incentive to get all done up for the classroom."

I knew Dad was looking at me, and concentrated on my battlements.

There was a pause.

"I heard," Mum said quietly, "she hasn't had an easy life. She had a fiancé . . . but parents, too. Not getting any younger . . . Too much responsibility for her young man. He upped and went."

Would that be with a canvas bag, like Alf, I wondered idly.

"She did her duty, stayed and nursed them. Now she's all alone. I don't think she can have many friends."

A teacher with friends! The very thought! I piled the mash a little higher.

"What with school and home, she wouldn't have time to socialise. That can't be good."

There was another pause.

"Go on," Dad said. "Admit it, Jane. You're missing it all, aren't you? Oh, I know you used to make a token protest when I brought another problem home, but you loved to do your bit, really."

I looked at Mum and caught her blush.

"And now it's you that's finding lame dogs for us!" Dad went on. "But I can't say that I mind," he added in a gentler voice. "This place is rather small, but we've still got love enough to make it big enough for one more.

"D'you think the turkey will stretch?"

Mum looked at him in consternation.

"I didn't think of that. Perhaps it's not too late to ask the butcher if he's got a bigger one . . ."

* * * *

Mr Poges, the butcher, ran his hands across his stripy-aproned front and eyed us solemnly.

"A bigger bird, eh, Mrs? Your young whippersnapper's found an appetite at last?"

He guffawed, and I shuffled uneasily. My life's ambition was to have muscles, and I could eat for Britain, but I never seemed to get beyond being gangly.

"Oh, no! We're going to have an extra guest for Christmas dinner. Miss Lacey from the school."

"Ah!" Mr Poges gave a wistful kind of sigh. "That's kind of you. Nice lady — so polite. Almost apologetic, now she has to ask me for a single chop. I can remember when she bought for three, of course, all those years."

He lapsed into a pensive silence, contemplating his poultry lying behind the pristine glass that closed his counter in.

"There's birds for every size of family," he went on, "bar single folk. Like her . . . And me. The festive season's not so festive when you're on your own."

The Lighthouse, Turnberry, Ayrshire

BUILT on a rocky promontory, with views west to the island of Ailsa Craig, this neat lighthouse stands close to the site of what was once Turnberry Castle. This was the probable birthplace of Robert I.

Now it is golfers who flock here, to play on Turnberry's two courses. Many famous players have battled with the fairways during championships held on the Turnberry links.

THE LIGHTHOUSE, TURNBERRY : J CAMPBELL KERR

"It's such a shame," Mum said, "to think of Mr Poges, who's made everybody else's Christmas so happy, being stuck with nothing but a bit of steak, and far-off memories of Mrs Poges! It's not as if he's got children he can go to."

"Well." Dad smiled as he fumbled in his wallet. "I can take a hint. And, if we haven't got the space we had, we kept the dining-table with the extra leaf, so *that'll* stretch.

"Mind you, I still recall that way you used to tut at me when I asked you to stretch things," he teased.

"I didn't really mean it," Mum said.

"I know." He slipped an arm around her waist and kissed her forehead. "It was a game we played."

"Between ourselves, George, not with people. We were serious enough about their welfare, weren't we?"

"Still are, I hope!"

W ELL, I was serious about presents and food at Christmas time — I wasn't into stretching mine. So it was rather comforting when Christmas came to realise they also stretched the other way.

Miss Lacey brought me shiny roller skates, and Mr Poges brought a football strip.

I would have worn them all to the meal if Mum hadn't been a rotten spoilsport. Worse, she made me sit between my oldest brothers, when what I really wanted was to sit between my teacher and the butcher, who were having such delightful little chats.

I couldn't hear a word from where I was but just the sight of them, their heads together, laughing, was so tantalising.

I demanded second helpings by way of recompense.

"The turkey *is* delicious," Mum remarked appreciatively.

"The very least I could do." Mr Poges suddenly went a bashful pink.

"Delicious," came the echo from Miss Lacey, and his cheeks went even redder.

I thought they'd never stop. Him going on about Miss Lacey's home-made Christmas pudding, and her all fluttery, not like a teacher at all. Why can't grown-ups act their age?

OK, it was a scrummy bird and a yummy pud, but couldn't they let it go at that?

I mean, they were still at it when my parents dragged the rest of us into the kitchen. How many does it take to make a pot of coffee?

And why were Mum and Dad congratulating one another and bursting out in giggles?

Why did Mum go quiet suddenly and misty-eyed when she mentioned Mr Poges and Miss Lacey would no doubt be seeing New Year in together?

Dad saw clean through her in that one.

"Can't bear a house that isn't stretched around the needy, Jane?"

"Rubbish!" she retorted, in a voice which wasn't fooling anyone.

I scraped the final scraps from all the plates into a bowl and beamed.

"Don't worry, Mum . . . I've found this dog. I put him in the garage yesterday. Fed him with my bedtime milk and biscuits, but I bet he's starving now. So you can feed him, if you like!"

I thought it was a pretty noble gesture on my part. The first lame dog I'd had for myself, and I was giving it to her!

She sighed dramatically.

"George, he's taking after you already."

"He's taking after both of us." Dad grinned, and Mum tutted like she used to.

"Am I never going to have a moment's peace?" she muttered, but she was smiling.

She didn't *want* a moment's peace. But maybe, I decided, as I ran a calculating eye across the turkey carcass, I should start learning to do a little stretching on my own account.

After all, she hadn't noticed that I'd taken those biscuits from the larder yesterday, together with an extra pint of milk. Of course, she would at suppertime . . .

I reckon that I did a tolerable imitation of the way Dad used to go about things.

"About this dog, Mum," I observed with casual composure. "Did I tell you that he's got a man with him? Remember Alf . . . ?"

* * * *

Funny, but I always do remember Alf at Christmas. He isn't with us any more, but there are so many like him at the shelter where I work.

Like Dad, I've turned collector, but professionally. And, just like Dad, I'm blessed to have found a wife like Mum, who stretches every small donation that we get.

Although the turkey's not a problem. Mr Poges, long retired, still buys us what we need each year. His way of saying thank you for the second Mrs Poges . . . ❑

IT was a crisp, clear night. From where my grandson, Joshua, and I were standing in the back garden, looking up at the stars, it seemed as if we could see the whole universe spread out before us like a giant map.

"All right, next question," I announced to the eleven-year-old boy beside me. "Where's Orion's Belt?"

Without hesitation, he pointed to the constellation, directing my gaze to the three stars which marked out the feature.

"That was an easy one, Grandad," he teased. "Come on, try again."

I smiled, knowing that it would be difficult to catch him out. Joshua knew all the constellations off by heart and our nightly study of the sky had ensured that he could easily pick them out of the jumbled mass of stars above us.

"What about the Pole Star?" I asked. "How do you find that?"

He frowned for a second, then brightened as he remembered.

"You follow the line of stars in the Great Bear — there it is!" he announced triumphantly. "Another one, Grandad!"

"Not now, lad. I think it's time we went in. We've been out here for half an hour and my toes are frozen!"

"But, Grandad . . ." He was always keen to stargaze just a little longer.

"No buts," I said sternly, then relented as his face fell. "But why don't you go through the encyclopaedia and learn about black holes? You can tell me all about them tomorrow."

As we turned to go in, he paused outside the back door and looked up at the earth's only satellite — the moon.

"Goodnight, sir," he said, as he always did, to the man in the moon. "See you tomorrow!"

Then, he scurried in to drag the encyclopaedia off the shelf and huddle in front of the fire with a cup of hot chocolate.

The ✶Moon✶

by Faye Robertson

Illustration by
Ewan McLeod.

Nature's Harvest

by John Taylor

IT was the back end of September and I was driving slowly — I never drive fast these days — on one of our back roads, when I spied some mushrooms in a field.

I know they weren't mine, but I had no qualms about mounting the dyke and picking them!

Anne is a dab hand at cooking mushrooms. She peels them, cuts them up into small pieces and puts them in a pan with some milk and boils them till tender. Then she adds flour, lots of pepper and salt, and some more milk and stirs until thick. We enjoy the mixture on toast.

Someone once asked me how I knew the mushrooms I picked in the fields were edible.

Somehow, I'd grown up knowing them. I'm speaking about what is called the common or field mushroom. I believe there are quite a number of species you can eat, but I only pick the field ones.

I made a pot of tea then joined him in the living-room. I deliberately kept out of the way of his mother, who was busy ironing his school uniform for the next day.

For a moment or two I watched him, amused, as he scoured the pages of the book. When he looked up at me, his face was dreamy and his eyes distant.

"Do you think I'll ever be an astronaut, Grandad?" he asked, hope filling his eager face.

I sipped my tea, cradling the mug in my hands.

"I think it's a distinct possibility," I replied and was rewarded with a bright grin.

I didn't miss his mother's warning glance as I continued.

"You just keep studying and learning. Some day it'll happen."

Anna folded up a shirt and put it on the pile by her side.

"Bed, Josh," she announced, beginning on a pair of trousers.

"But, Mum . . ."

"Now, Josh. You've got school in the morning."

ONE Tuesday, I was in Cupar on my own and went for a meander round a small supermarket.

I noticed a counter which had items whose sell-by date was there and then. There was a large basket of mushrooms. They looked firm to me but I knew they would have to be dealt with that night. Less than a quarter the normal price . . .

Muggins bought them and expected, when I put them on the kitchen table, to be asked who was going to deal with them. But, for once, I'd done something right!

"Thank you, John! Those are my answer."

Answer to what?

On the coming Sunday I knew we were going to skip church, a thing we rarely do, and drive up for lunch to our daughter and son-in-law's farm in Perthshire.

Anne, all her life, has been one for giving rather than receiving. She doesn't like to go, even visiting our daughter, without taking something.

"I'll make mushroom soup for Sunday for Mary."

That evening we made enough mushroom soup to do ten folk, although there would only be four of us for lunch on Sunday.

"Why make so much?" I asked.

"It'll save Mary during the week." Anne has an answer for everything.

Well, it was gratefully received and enjoyed by all. There's nothing like a real taste of the countryside.

The Farmer And His Wife

He gave an exaggerated sigh as he placed his encyclopaedia carefully on the shelf, then saluted me in our usual parting manner.

"Beam me up, Scottie," he instructed, adding a cheeky grin as he ran up the stairs.

"Over and out," I countered, wishing I could move half as quickly as he could!

Anna and I sat in silence for a while, she ironing and me sipping my tea.

I could picture Joshua, sitting up in bed, studying his model of the space shuttle. Until his mother went to tuck him in and turn out his light, that is. But then, long after he was supposed to be asleep, he would study his *Map of the Heavens* chart under the bedclothes by torchlight!

"What's up?" I asked, aware that, from some reason, Anna was annoyed with me.

"You shouldn't encourage him," she scolded, folding the trousers neatly.

"Why on earth not?" I was puzzled.

"Because he's going to be a very disappointed young boy one day."

"Why?" I persisted stubbornly.

"Oh, Dad." She sighed. "You know there's no way he'll ever be an astronaut."

"I wonder if Neil Armstrong's mum ever said that."

She was forced to laugh.

"Well, don't blame me when he comes down to earth with a bump."

"Let him dream his dreams," I told her, as I put on my jacket to go home. "You never know, they might just come true."

I GAVE the conversation little thought for the following week, as I was busy in the garden, preparing the beds for their spring flowering. I was, in fact, in the middle of weed clearing when the phone went.

"Hello?" I couldn't think who could be calling me at this time of day. Anna was at work, and most of my friends lived nearby and tended to pop round rather than ring.

"Dad?" It was Anna, sounding more than a little frantic. "I was just about to hang up — I thought you were out."

"I'm here, love. Calm down and tell me what's happened."

"It's Josh." She stopped, unable to continue.

I went cold as a hundred different possibilities flitted through my head.

"Is he OK?"

"He's in hospital. He was taken from school by an ambulance. He's had some sort of asthma attack."

"Asthma?" I sighed, feeling sorry for the boy, knowing only too well what it was like to suffer from it. "Do you want me to come up?"

"Can you? Rob's away in London and I can't get hold of him. I'd just like someone here . . ."

"I'll leave now," I told her, writing down the name of Joshua's ward before ringing off.

It took me no time to get ready and I was at the hospital within 15 minutes of Anna's call.

I pondered on Joshua's attack as I hurried through the hospital, looking for the ward he was in. I had suffered badly from asthma as a child and still had an inhaler somewhere in the house, although I hadn't used it for some time.

Anna had somehow managed to escape its clutches and we had thought that it had by-passed Josh, too — until now.

I asked a nurse to direct me to Josh's bed and found Anna sitting by his side, watching him.

"Thanks for coming, Dad."

"That's all right," I said. "I'm glad I was there when you rang.

"How is he? Is he still feeling bad, Anna?"

I looked at Joshua, who was turned on his side away from me, his face hidden in the pillow.

"He's better now," she said. "They put him on something called a nebuliser — like an oxygen mask, over his face, to help him breathe."

"What brought it on?" I asked, puzzled.

"Apparently he's had wheezy spells for some while, but just thought it was general breathlessness, after he'd been running. He said it was worse over the winter, but he just thought it was the cold. I honestly never noticed any sign of it."

I sighed, walking round the bed to sit in front of Joshua. He must have known I was there, but refused to look at me.

"Houston," I said, quoting a line from the Apollo 13 mission, "we have a problem."

Joshua had seen the film of the flight nine times and the saying would usually have raised a smile from him but he said nothing now, merely sniffling into the pillow.

"What's up?" I persisted. "Still feeling poorly?"

He shook his head, then turned to face me. I saw that his eyes were all blotchy; he'd obviously been crying.

"I've got asthma," he said in a hushed voice.

"I know. But it's not the end of the world," I replied. "I've got it, too, and it's not a problem as long as you learn to control it. Come on, Josh. You'll be fine — "

"But I can't be an astronaut now!" He buried his head back into the pillow, sobbing loudly.

The penny dropped and I closed my eyes, realising why he was so upset.

H E was right, of course. As he grew up, there might well be times when it got better, or even disappeared for a while, but I knew that there was no real cure for the problem.

To be an astronaut you would have to be at the peak of fitness. Even if the asthma appeared to be better, they would never let him go into space with the risk that he might have an attack.

I opened my eyes and saw that Anna was watching me with tears in her eyes, her face flushed.

"It's your fault," she snapped, bottom lip trembling. "I told you not to encourage him. Now look what you've done."

We both looked at Joshua, who was sobbing his heart out into the pillow.

"I'd better go," I said to Anna, knowing that I was not the person she needed at that moment.

"Dad . . ."

But I left, knowing that there was nothing I could say.

WHEN I got home, I sat in the garden and went over the situation again and again in my mind. For a while I wallowed in self pity, flooded with guilt and regret. If only I hadn't encouraged Joshua!

But we all have dreams when we are young. Every boy wants to be a train driver or a fighter pilot.

But we usually have time to grow out of our dreams — Joshua had been rudely awoken from his.

I thought of my grandson's tears, and knew that I'd been right to encourage his interests — but wrong not to suggest some other, simpler, careers he could follow.

Then, almost as if she were standing before me, I heard my wife telling me not to feel sorry for myself. I'd have to go and do something positive to put things right!

"You're right, Patty," I said out loud, "and I wish you were here to help me out of this one. But it's my fault Joshua's so upset — and it's up to me to make it better for him."

I went inside, an idea forming in my head, and fetched the local papers from the magazine rack by my chair. Then I sat down to pore through them.

The next day, I made my way to the hospital, a box under my arm.

I'd spoken to Anna the night before and she had explained that she hadn't meant what she'd said. She had just been upset and worried about Josh.

I had replied that I understood perfectly and then I told her of my idea. She'd been pleased, and said that Joshua would love it.

But as I walked down the white corridors, I felt suddenly nervous. Anna had said that Joshua was still upset and I wasn't as sure as she was that my ruse would work.

Finding his bed, I felt an initial surge of joy when I saw him sitting up reading a comic. He seemed as fit and healthy as usual, but then I saw his miserable face.

"Hello," I said. "You're looking better. I hear you're coming out tonight."

"Yes, with loads of sprays and things." His face was sulky.

"I'm sorry about that," I replied softly. "And I'm sorry you can't be an astronaut now. But you must count your blessings; you're going to be fine providing you take care of yourself."

"I know," he mumbled.

"Did you hear that an amateur astronomer has discovered a new planet?"

I could see the interest flare in his eyes, although he tried to look nonchalant and merely shrugged.

"No-one had seen it before, not even the experts. He's going to have it named after him. Imagine that, Josh! That planet will still be there in

A Century of Change

Happy And Glorious!

ALL the pomp and ceremony of the Queen's Coronation will live long in the memories of those waiting in the cold and wet on the route to Westminster Abbey on June 2, 1953. There was awe as the Golden Coach swept along, pulled by eight grey horses.

And no-one could forget the beaming Queen of Tonga as she enjoyed her ride to the ceremony.

Millions watched on TV or listened to the radio commentary as the oath of accession was taken and Queen Elizabeth II was proclaimed head of the British Commonwealth.

Queen Elizabeth II was just twenty-seven, married, with two young children — four-year-old Charles and two-year-old Anne.

© Associated Press

The Coronation captured the public imagination and there were parties all around the country and souvenirs galore. There was a real feeling of optimism after the shortages and hardships following the war.

As her sister, Princess Margaret, is reported to have said: "The Coronation was like a phoenix-time. Everything was being raised from the ashes. There was this gorgeous-looking, lovely young lady and nothing to stop anything getting better and better."

1950–1959

hundreds of years — what a legacy!"

He put down his comic, too excited now to pretend not to be interested.

"Oh, Grandad, I wish I could do something like that!"

"Well," I said, "as it happens, I've got something here that might help you do just that."

I put the box on to his bed.

He stared at it for a moment, then eagerly ripped it open, quickly

Hebridean Gem *by Brenda G. Macrow*

I KNOW an island in the west
  Where warm sea breezes blow,
And the mists that crown the
  Cuillin's crest
  Pour to the glens below.

Rain sweeps over the jagged heights,
  Then, in a breath, is gone,
And a thousand scintillating lights
  Dance in the dazzling sun.

Turquoise the sea, with purple w
  Golden the shifting sand —
Beauty that fills our deepest need
  Blossoms on every hand.

Gem of the haunted Hebrides,
  A dream that will not die —
Haven of peace and sweet heart'
  ease,
The misty Isle of Skye.

parting the football wrapping paper I'd found in the hospital gift shop.

"Oh, Grandad," he whispered, lifting it carefully out of the box, his eyes wide in surprise and delight. "It's fantastic!"

It was a telescope, polished and gleaming. On the side it was engraved: *Joshua Kent.*

"It's got my name on it," he gasped.

"That's because it's yours." I smiled. "It's only second hand, but it's a good one and it'll help you to see a lot more stars than you can with the naked eye.

"Perhaps we can turn your mum's attic into an observation tower — if your mum doesn't mind, that is . . ."

He looked at me, then threw his arms around my neck and gave me a fierce hug.

"It's wonderful." He was beaming now. "Thanks, Grandad!" He was eagerly examining his present.

"I know you can't go to the moon now," I said, a little awkwardly, "but there's still hundreds of jobs you can do in astronomy."

"I wouldn't mind staying an amateur if I discovered a planet!" he announced cheerfully.

I grinned back. I was glad to see that the stars were, finally, back in his eyes — where they belonged. ❑

Sgurr nan Gillean, Skye.

Dennis Hardley.

Illustration by John Hancock.

by Jane O'Hare

WHEN Kate came back on duty there was a screen around Miss Dudnam's bed. The heart specialist was examining her, accompanied by Sister Nock. What verdict was Mr Manley likely to pass on her dear little landlady?

As soon as Sister was free, Kate asked her.

"She's not too good," Sister said, "but with care . . . we'll see.

"Someone special to you, Miss Dudnam, isn't she? Ah, well . . ."

Sister's way of leaving sentences unfinished might be irritating, yet she knew all her nurses' home backgrounds. Their joys and sorrows mattered to her. And she guessed Kate had spent a disturbed weekend with her parents.

When Two Hearts Beat As One

What she didn't know was that Nick had let Kate down, again, and that they'd parted, permanently this time.

Last Friday, an hour before they'd been due to set off for the long-delayed first meeting between Nick and Kate's parents, he'd come round to tell her that he couldn't make it. Again. A vital sales trip had cropped up.

Already distressed over the heart attack which had brought Miss Dudnam on to her ward earlier in the day, Kate had asked him the question point-blank.

"Do you really want to meet my parents? Or, do you feel that if you meet them, you'll be making too much of a commitment?"

Few people could meet the direct gaze of Kate Baxter and lie. Nick, who loved and respected her, didn't even try.

She was the only woman he'd ever wanted permanently in his life, he said, but not with marriage vows, a mortgage and a house in suburbia . . .

His sales career meant travelling all over the world. If he hadn't made director by the time he was thirty-five, he might as well resign. He didn't intend that to happen to him.

Kate had tried to hide how much he'd hurt her.

"I'm a country girl, Nick, from a loving family background. I was brought up to believe in marriage . . . and in freedom within that marriage for both partners to grow. Perhaps, have children."

They'd stared at each other, both hurt, both stunned by what was happening.

"I hoped it wouldn't come to this, Kate," he'd said. "I don't want us to part. You know I love you, don't you? And respect your dedication to nursing.

"We're both dedicated. With so much in common we could have a good life together . . ."

But she'd drawn away, shaking her head. She knew herself too well. She'd never cease to want the happy permanence her parents had.

So she'd gone home alone to her parents. She'd spent some of that interminable weekend with her childhood sweetheart, who'd been waiting for her ever since she'd gone to London to nurse. Not that Kate had encouraged him.

It was soothing to be with Richard, but throughout the whole time her heart had ached.

Now it was Monday and she was back doing the work she loved, caring for the sick, with her own healthy heart beating sadly inside her . . .

But when she slipped round the screen to see her landlady, her calm face betrayed none of her inner pain.

"Hello, Kate, dear," Miss Dudnam said quietly. "I've been longing to see you, to know how things went this weekend. I couldn't sleep until I had . . ."

Kate checked her pulse automatically.

"You've had a bad weekend, Duddie. You need sleep more than anything."

Miss Dudnam's face lightened at the affectionate nickname.

"It was your special weekend, and Nick's. How did the family like him?"

Kate was tempted to lie but she couldn't.

"Nick couldn't spare the time again, Duddie. So I asked him if he really wanted to meet them." She shook her head. "Marriage isn't on, for Nick, so we've split up. Permanently, I suppose . . ."

"Oh, my dear, I am sorry. You must feel so hurt. Both of you." She lay quietly for a moment, then opened her eyes and gazed at Kate.

"I can't believe you've parted for ever, though. Fate meant you both to be together, and you will be."

Kate nodded, anxiously aware of her patient's weakness.

"You must sleep now, Duddie," she said firmly, and Duddie smiled.

"While I do, you remember, Kate, how fate brought the three of us together . . . There has to be a reason for that."

Kate left her sleeping, and though it was a busy day, her thoughts often strayed to that first meeting Duddie had spoken of.

IT had been soon after she'd finished her final exams. On an off-duty day, she'd been searching the city for an affordable bed-sitter. In a quiet area of tall, Edwardian houses, she was looking for a bus stop when she heard the screech of brakes and a cry.

Running towards the sound, she saw a car with the driver's door hanging open, and a dark young man helping an elderly woman to the pavement.

"I'm a nurse," Kate panted as she reached them. "Can I help?"

"Would you, please?" The man looked concerned. "I stopped in time, so she's not hurt. But she's shocked —"

"My own fault," the elderly woman said breathlessly. "I stepped right in front of this poor man's car —"

Kate could see her lips had a blue tinge.

"The best thing is to get you home. Do you live nearby?"

"Just there." She pointed to the end house.

"You need to rest and you need some hot, sweet tea. Have you got anyone who can make it for you?"

The old lady shook her head.

"Would you like me to come in? My name's Kate, Kate Baxter. I'm off duty all day —"

"And my name is Everitt. Nick Everitt." The young man took a business card from an inside pocket and held it out for them both to see. "This is me, and I assure you I'm very trustworthy!"

"I'm Miss Dudnam. Agnes Dudnam. Let's all have tea, if Nurse Kate will be kind enough to make it?"

Between them they got her indoors, and Kate left her on the settee, chatting with the young man — Nick — while she made tea in the spacious kitchen.

When she'd served tea all round, Kate sat down opposite them. For the first time, her eyes met Nick Everitt's and her heart lurched.

His eyes were the deepest brown she'd ever seen, and as they gazed back into her own, a great ripple of awareness swept her body, leaving her tingling and breathless.

She knew instantly that something precious was happening. And she knew with a strange certainty that it had happened to him, too . . .

"Nick has just been telling me about his last trip to Hong Kong. He's a sales executive, dear. And I was telling him about myself." Miss Dudnam sounded brighter now.

"I nursed Mother for most of my life, so I've never married, although there was someone, once." She smiled at Nick, and sipped her tea.

"No ring, I see. So you're single, too? Nick isn't married either, he tells me . . ."

Kate felt a stab of embarrassment. Was the old lady matchmaking? But what if she was?

Kate suddenly realised she was hoping Miss Dudnam got her way!

Gordon Henderson.

THEY chatted on for some minutes, then Nick suddenly glanced at the clock.

"Good heavens! I must go, but I must say I've enjoyed meeting you both, despite the disastrous start. Could I — offer you a lift, Nurse — er, Kate?"

Kate hesitated, wanting very much to say yes, but aware of the disappointment on Miss Dudnam's face.

"I'd like to stay a bit longer with Miss Dudnam, thank you, Nick," her kind heart prompted her to say.

She didn't imagine it — he pulled a mock-frustrated face.

"Right," he said, in the decisive way she was to come to love. "I have to fly to Munich, but I shall be back tomorrow. Do you have a free evening soon, Kate? I'd very much like to take you out to dinner."

Just as decisively, she said she'd love that, and after they arranged when and where to meet, he shook Miss Dudnam's hand.

"Can I call and see you again, too, Miss Dudnam? Next week, say?"

After Nick had gone, Miss Dudnam felt well enough to pour the second cup of tea herself, and to ask Kate what she was doing in the area. And when Kate had told her, she said eagerly, "Do you believe in fate, Nurse?"

"If you mean do I believe everything which happens to us is fixed, no, I don't. Although I do think it seems as if we're led a certain way, sometimes . . ."

"Exactly!" Miss Dudnam said, eyes sparkling. "And today, you and Nick were led to me.

"Especially you, Kate, because I can supply what you need most at this time in your life!" She paused, then rushed on.

"I've just realised that the top half of this house could easily be converted into a flat . . . Would you be interested in taking it, if it were?"

Summer's End

MELLOW season, when summer days have fled,
Of ripened fruits and berries on the briar —
The waving woods now flaunt their gold and red,
While bracken sets the sombre braes afire.

Now nights are still, and frost is in the air.
A huge, bright moon sails dreamily on high.
The harvest's in, the stubble fields are bare,
And Turner sunsets paint the western sky.

A bittersweet nostalgia stirs the heart,
A sadness for the golden summer's end —
Yet, in this magic season, set apart,
Warm shades of rust and orange boldly blend
To deck the hills with autumn colours bright
And touch the first, frail snows with dancing light.
— *Brenda G. Macrow.*

n Eighe, Wester Ross.

Would she be interested! Kate was over the moon, especially when she saw what she was being offered. They agreed on it right away.

The next few months were wonderful. That first evening spent with Nick had been another dream come true.

They'd gone to a Greek restaurant, and eaten moussaka and drunk red wine, and enjoyed music which made their hearts dance. Music turned out to be just one of many shared interests they'd discovered.

They'd also discovered that when they touched hands or looked into each other's eyes, they'd felt an instant, mutual delight . . . Kate soon knew she was deeply in love for the first time. The only time for her, because that was how she was made.

Nick loved her. He told her it was the first time for him, as well. Yet there was a reserve in him — she sensed it, and it should have made her wary. She guessed it came from his ambition, his determination to get to the top in his job . . .

One evening, after dining and dancing, they'd returned to Kate's much-loved flatlet at Duddie's. Sitting together, soft music playing, she'd nestled her head into his shoulder.

"Ambition makes you restless, doesn't it? You rarely sit still for long, yet you don't seem to suffer from stress at all. I do wonder, though, if you won't find it hard to relax once you've reached the top . . ."

He'd kissed her hair.

"Dear Kate. Don't fret about my health, I'm as fit as a fiddle. Some people thrive on stress, and perhaps I'm one of them.

"You make the top sound like a very uncomfortable peak," he'd added. "But it won't be like that. I'll still be on the move because there'll still be challenges. Different challenges, but just as exciting."

"You mean you'll be travelling all your life, in one way or another?"

"Yes." He'd looked surprised. "Isn't everyone doing that, in their own particular way?"

She'd agreed that life was a journey. But some people, like Nick, travelled too fast and missed happiness on the way . . .

If she'd said it aloud, that night, a lot of things might have been different. But life, Kate thought, was too full and too good to risk it all . . .

I SHOULD have been on my guard. I shouldn't have let myself love him so much, Kate thought as she worked on the ward. But how could anyone stop themselves from loving too much? All she could do now was bury her heart. If she ignored the pain, perhaps it would grow less.

She thought of the day when Miss Dudnam had brought up the subject of fate again.

"What made you become a nurse?" she'd asked. So Kate had told her about Richard's accident. Duddie already knew about Richard.

"We were playing by the fence at the bottom of the garden, jumping off, and Richard caught his wrist on a spiky piece of wood. You should have seen the blood!

"I remembered hearing of a man who'd bled to death because he'd cut an artery. So I tore off my hair ribbons, and bound Richard's arm above the cut." She laughed. "That was when I decided I'd be a nurse one day."

"But that's fate, directing you," Duddie exclaimed. "I never told you how I came to step in front of Nick's car, did I?"

Kate shook her head.

"I had a sudden feeling that something wonderful was about to occur, just as I stepped off the kerb . . . Luckily Nick stopped, and then the three of us met up in that wonderful way . . ."

"It was a dangerous thing to do," Kate said severely, and Miss Dudnam nodded agreement.

"You're right. That's what David said to me the day we met. Mother and I were on holiday in Brighton, and I did the same thing in front of his car.

"I'd felt that same feeling, and I was drawn towards this man, sitting in traffic in an open-topped car.

"He told me off, but not too much because we were drawn to one another . . . We were in Brighton for a whole month and for the rest of the time he came to see me every day . . ." She sighed.

"He wanted to continue our friendship after we returned home, but

Mother was very upset. She was a semi-invalid even then, you see, and needed me . . . So that was that."

"I'm so sorry," Kate said gently, her warm heart touched.

"There's no need." Duddie smiled. "Perhaps I had the best of it. A happy meeting, a brief magic, then a fond memory for all time . . .

"I've always been content with my life, but I do believe in fate, and I'm sure you and Nick were meant for each other . . ."

It seemed they weren't, though, Kate thought now as she carried on with her duties. Any more than she and Richard had been meant for each other . . .

Yesterday afternoon, the two of them had gone for a walk along the riverside. It was a walk both knew well, and they'd walked along in silence until suddenly Richard asked why she was so low.

She glanced at him, then away again, knowing she couldn't tell him about Nick. Not now, perhaps not ever. So she'd told him about Duddie's heart attack, and, for the first time, about her landlady's belief in fate.

"Her belief in fate beckoned her in front of a car?" Richard snorted. "Oh, Kate! No wonder you're feeling off colour these days — you're living with a nutcase! A nice nutcase, I daresay, but a nutcase all the same!"

That down-to-earth reaction was typical of him, but his words had jarred. At that moment she'd seen Richard — really seen him — as the practical young farmer he was. Someone she'd shared a happy childhood affection with, but someone she'd grown away from.

After that, she'd got Richard to accept at last that they should remain friends, no more.

It had been a weekend of partings, she thought, making her way to Duddie's bed. Just as she reached the screen, Sister handed her a huge bunch of white chrysanths.

"Gorgeous, aren't they? They're for your Miss Dudnam. Want to take them to her?"

Kate nodded, reading the card attached to the bouquet.

Watching over you . . . It was unsigned.

Duddie was fast asleep.

Kate knew she shouldn't — there weren't enough nursing hours in the day to go round — but she put the flowers in water and left them where Duddie could see them.

At six, Kate took a last peep around the screen before going off duty, and found the patient lying awake.

"How do you feel?" She went over to her bedside.

"Well rested, but a little tired." Duddie nodded at the flowers. "Thank you for those, my dear. They're lovely."

"But I didn't send them! I only arranged them." She picked up the card and read its message, and the elderly lady sighed happily.

"That's all it needs to say," she murmured. "They're from Nick, dear. And his flowers say it all, for the romantic man he is . . . White lanterns, they are . . . Lanterns of hope for you, and for me . . ."

Kate blinked back sudden, unexpected tears.

Outside the hospital, rush hour was over, but the traffic still roared past as she set off for the Underground.

A T first, she failed to notice the car on the opposite side of the street. But then, above the clamour of traffic, something made her glance across. To meet Nick's eyes, to see his hand raised from the steering-wheel to wave.

Without thinking, she moved to the edge of the pavement.

"No, Kate! Wait!" His frantic shout stopped her. He shot out of the car and sprinted across to her.

Breathlessly he gripped her shoulders.

"Oh, Kate! I thought for a terrible moment you were going to do just what Duddie did —"

Shuddering, he held her against him, almost crushing her in relief.

Soon they were sitting together in his car. For some reason, her head was on his shoulder. Cradling her, he took her hands in his.

"Before we say anything else, Kate, please tell me something vitally important. I love you, and I want us to get married. Will you?"

"You want us to marry because that's the only way to get me to stay?" she said, but he shook his head.

"No. I want us to get married because I can't live without you, and I want the whole world to know it."

She sat dazed, hardly daring to acknowledge the joy inside her.

"Yes," she said at last. "Yes, I'll marry you . . . But why did you change your mind?"

"I didn't." His arms tightened round her. "I just didn't realise until we weren't seeing each other any more how much I wanted to be married to you. Ever since we met I've felt so wonderful inside, as if I was in tune with you, and the whole universe . . . Then, when we parted, the feeling left me. And it was terrible!"

They kissed then, and Kate could hardly breathe. She knew it was all right now. Fate had taken a hand.

"You sent the flowers to Duddie, didn't you Nick? And that message . . ."

"Yes," he said simply. "It was meant for both of you."

"Duddie understood. And she's over the worst, now."

"Sister said, when I rang up. The worst's over for us, too, isn't it? We know where we're going now, don't we?"

"Yes, oh yes, we do . . ."

Kate had never felt so much happiness in her life. She couldn't wait to tell Duddie she'd been right all along.

They *were* meant to be together, she and Nick . . . together for ever. ❏

Illustration by Mike Heslop.

Alone At Last!

MARIAN knew this was the right house the moment she saw it. It wasn't particularly grand, or steeped in history, but she knew it was for them. The children wouldn't even have to change schools. It needed a lot of work, but the structure was sound, which was all that really mattered.

She fell in love with the large square kitchen, the morning room that captured every single ray of sun, and the en-suite bathroom which meant that she didn't have to queue behind Helen every morning.

by Joyce Begg

The garden was all lawn and trees, with a barbecue, tubs for flowers placed strategically on the patio and, at the far end, a summerhouse of seasoned wood on a rotating base.

She loved everything, even the ancient central-heating boiler and the cellar that seemed to be a breeding ground for all types of spider!

"The thing is," Bill had said earnestly, once they had signed on the dotted line, "we won't be able to afford a holiday this year. You do understand, Marian?"

"Yes, dear," Marian said, mentally patting his head. "I know exactly how much it cost, and the size of the mortgage. Even I can work out that a holiday is out of the question."

Once they had moved in, however, the holiday issue raised its head again.

"You mean we're not going *anywhere*?" Helen, at fourteen, assumed that holidays were a natural part of life's progression, like Christmas, and exams. Not having a holiday was like not getting a birthday present. Unthinkable!

"Not this year," her mother said cheerfully. "The new house has cost a great deal more than just an arm and a leg."

"But what am I going to tell Stephanie?" Helen blanched. "They're going to Lanzarote."

"I'm sure you'll think of something."

Eleven-year-old Toby was strangely unconcerned about holidays, so long as he got to the scout weekend.

"Mike says there were millions of insects in the tent last year," he announced with relish.

"Really?" Marian smiled. "Tell him he can camp in our cellar any time he likes."

THROUGHOUT the weeks of early summer, Marian worked solidly on the house. The moment she came in from her part-time job in the craft centre, she would set about the paintwork, sew up curtains, cut out lino tiles.

Bill felt even worse about the non-existent holiday.

"Please don't work so hard. You're making me feel dreadful. Where's my golf sweater?" he went on.

"It's washed and ironed, ready for your weekend away. Wear something else just now."

"Oh. All right."

The golf weekend, an annual event that Bill enjoyed with his mates, was about to coincide with the scout camp, which would leave Helen and Marian on their own.

"We'll do some nice girly things," Marian promised, by way of compensation. "We may not be able to afford a holiday, but I'm sure we can rise to some jeans and T-shirts. Maybe do lunch in a posh restaurant as well. What do you say, Helen?"

"You've forgotten, Mum. It's my geography field trip. We're supposed to be going to the Peak District. You're right about the jeans, though. I'll need them by next Saturday."

"Oh. Right. I see." She realised she sounded a little forlorn, but no-one else noticed.

"You surely don't intend to wear new jeans to crawl over rocks, do you?" she said, ever practical. "Wear the ones with the patches. Then you can be practical and devastatingly attractive at the same time."

THE Friday they were all due to leave on their various trips came around at last, and Marian had them all organised down to the last sock. This was when they finally realised that she was going to be on her own!

"I'm sorry, love." Bill was stricken. "I didn't think."

"I can go, can't I, Mum?" Toby asked anxiously. "You'll be all right, won't you?"

And Helen was determined.

"*I* can't stay at home. This is part of my geography course," she told her parents quickly.

"You could visit my mother, if you like," Bill said helpfully. "That would pass an afternoon for you."

"You could paint my bedroom," Toby chipped in. "Black, remember."

"And I'd like lots of cushions for mine, Mum," Helen added. "Not too frilly."

Marian smiled blandly at them, saying nothing at all. Then, before they could come up with any other ideas, a van drew up outside and they heard a horn peep.

"That's your lift, Toby," his mother said, and gave him a swift hug before any of his friends could see.

The next one off was Helen, and then Bill.

She was alone at last!

Saturday morning dawned bright and sunny, with the lightest of breezes. Marian had a leisurely breakfast, accompanied by a little Mozart, and then put on her newest T-shirt, a long cotton skirt, and comfortable sandals. By half-past ten, everything was ready. She switched on the answering machine, closed the doors behind her, and set off.

The smell of roses and carnations followed her down the garden all the way to the summerhouse, already warmed by the sun. There was the lounger, and the cool bag with its salads and its winebox. And there, on the ledge, were her sunglasses and a fat new paperback.

Who needed a family holiday when she could have two whole days of blissful idle solitude in the summerhouse? ❏

Glen Etive, Argyll

THE entrance at the north end of this glen is guarded by the mountain Buachaille Etive Mor — the Shepherd Of Etive. It is a long, twisting road which takes the motorist along the River Etive and south to Loch Etive — a narrow loch sandwiched between towering hills and overshadowed by Ben Cruachan. The Cruachan power station, to the south of the glen, is well worth a visit. Here you are invited to travel into the heart of the mountain!

Loch Etive stretches south to Taynuilt and beyond to Connel Bridge where it flows into the sea at the Falls of Lora.

GLEN ETIVE, ARGYLL : J CAMPBELL KERR

The Lilac Suit

by Jennie Cairns

AS Annie Campbell caught sight of the familiar lilac suit, she blinked in surprise. The unknown wearer was tall and slim. Annie glanced down at her own ample figure and sighed, but quietly, because she was in church.

Not that this was a normal service. It was a wedding.

She craned her neck to follow the progress of the suit and, at the same time, eased herself on the hard pew. A seat with a cushion would have been a more comfortable choice.

She couldn't see the face of the person wearing the lilac, just a wealth of very fair hair bouncing on slender shoulders. She must be a guest, because she was near the front; unlike Annie, who was at the back. She was there just to see the wedding of that nice girl in the post office.

Annie liked weddings. Once she would have gone upstairs to the gallery for a better view but now those twisting, stone stairs made her think twice.

On this occasion, though, Annie found herself paying little heed to the bride. Her attention was focused on the figure in lilac near the front.

That suit had hung in her own wardrobe, unworn, for years, only to be taken out occasionally, pressed and put back again. Annie was sentimental about it.

How Dave would have laughed. But Dave hadn't been with her to laugh for a good long time now.

He would have laughed especially if he had seen her holding the dress against herself. Had she ever been able to fit into that narrow waist? When she slipped on the jacket, it was tight in the shoulders and wouldn't fasten across her chest, not by inches.

Trying it on had been a depressing experience, requiring an

immediate cup of tea and a sit down.

It was at that moment she finally made up her mind what she was going to do. The next day, the suit, once again pressed and this time folded carefully, was handed in at the charity shop in the High Street.

"It's lovely," the woman behind the counter said.

Annie nodded.

"It's very plain, a simple dress and fitted jacket, with mother-of-pearl buttons. I bought it years ago and I've always liked it, but now it just doesn't fit."

"I know the feeling." The woman smiled. "Too many inches in the wrong place. It happens to us all!"

W HEN the bridal party came down the aisle, Annie stood up with the rest of the congregation, but her attention still wasn't on the bride, but on the progress of her lilac suit. Its wearer reached the end of Annie's pew and she caught a glimpse of blue eyes and a smiling face.

The outfit looked remarkably good. No-one would have guessed its age. But then, it certainly was the most expensive she had ever bought.

Annie followed the crowd out on to the church steps. The fair-haired young woman was now, like the other guests, throwing handfuls of confetti. That would certainly annoy the church officer when he had to sweep it up.

There was a lot of laughter and chatter and more than a little pushing. Annie found herself swept too near the steps. She lost her balance and grabbed at the person nearest her.

Horrified, she watched as the wearer of the lilac suit stumbled and slid in an ungainly heap to the bottom of the three shallow steps leading down to the gravel path.

"I'm sorry. I'm so sorry!" Annie cried, regaining her own balance. "It was all my fault."

"It's my ankle —" The girl was gasping, her face white under the gleaming hair.

Annie found herself pushed further back in the crowd and leaned gratefully against the grey stone of the church. Someone helped the sufferer into a car and she was driven off.

Annie slipped back into the church to sit alone until all the guests were gone and then walked miserably home.

Her pleasure in seeing the lilac suit was gone. All she could think of was the wearer's white face as she was helped into a car, leaning heavily on the supporting arm of some young man.

She was troubled for the rest of the day and slept badly.

The next day she made a trip to the post office and mentioned the accident to another member of the counter staff, trying to hide her awkwardness.

A CENTURY OF CHANGE

"One Small Step For Man . . ."

ONE giant leap for mankind."
These were the words of Neil Armstrong, the first man to set foot on the moon, at 3.56 a.m. British Summer Time on July 21, 1969. And he looked like he was having fun, floating with each step.

The climax of the Apollo 11 mission came four days after blast-off from Cape Kennedy. After orbiting the moon, Armstrong and fellow astronaut Edwin "Buzz" Aldrin transferred to the lunar module, Eagle, to prepare for their descent. A few minutes later, the announcement came: "The Eagle has landed."

Press Association Photos

Armstrong and Aldrin both obviously enjoyed their walk on the moon and collected samples and planted the American flag.

Armstrong reported that the moon's surface was covered in a fine powder, "like some desert in the United States". And, as there was no wind to blow the powder or rain to wash it away, his footprints will remain there for ever.

• • • • • • • • • 1960 – 1969 • • • • • • • • • •

"Do you happen to know who the young girl was?" Annie asked.

"Oh, that was Susie Morton, the bride's cousin. Don't you know Susie?"

"Is she all right?"

"Chipped a bone in her foot, I hear. She's in plaster."

"Oh, dear." Annie lifted her postage stamps and began to turn away. "I feel awful. It was my fault. I pushed her — accidentally, of course."

"Your change, Mrs Campbell! You've forgotten it." The assistant caught Annie as she opened the shop door.

"Thanks," Annie said faintly and took herself off.

It wasn't really entirely her fault. It was the fault of that lilac suit! She wished with all her heart she'd left it hanging in the wardrobe, where it belonged. One thing she did hope, though — that she would never see it again, or its wearer.

LATER that week she answered her doorbell and found a visitor, a young woman dressed in jeans and a white sweater, with curly blonde hair streaming over her shoulders.

Annie's dismayed gaze took in the plaster and the walking stick.

"Hello." The smile was wide and friendly, the blue eyes smiling.

"I came to let you know I'm perfectly all right. Jean in the post office told me you were worried and gave me your address."

"Please come in and sit down." Annie pulled the door open.

"I've been feeling so guilty. You see, it was the suit. I wanted to see it close up —" She broke off in confusion.

Susie Morton sank into a chair and pushed her walking stick behind her heels on the floor.

"Pretty good, wasn't it? Much admired. You'll never guess where I bought it. In the charity shop! I saw it in the window and all I had to do was shorten the skirt."

"I knew where you'd bought it." Annie straightened her shoulders. "You see, I'd handed it in."

"You did?" The blue eyes widened and sparkled with amusement. "No wonder you wanted a good look at it on me. I hope you approved!"

Annie found she was relaxing and decided at that moment the occasion called for a cup of tea.

"Mind you, I still feel guilty that I was responsible for you falling and doing that —" She pointed at the plaster.

"Please, don't. It's an ill wind that blows nobody good, as my granny says. Jim Steele, that fellow who ran me to the doctor — I've seen quite a bit of him since. I think he fancies me and, well —" Her smile widened. "I kind of fancy him!"

Fancies me! What a way to express it, Annie thought as she filled the kettle. A different way of saying it all right, but surely the same old meaning.

She brought the tea things into the sitting-room.

"I was married in that suit," she said suddenly.

"Were you really?"

"Yes. Who knows? Maybe you . . .?"

As Annie's voice trailed off, the girl threw back her head and laughed, her blonde hair bouncing on her shoulders.

Annie joined in the laughter and it seemed to her that she felt young again, almost as young as when she wore that lilac suit all those years ago and Dave was whispering in her ear.

"I do love you in lilac!" ❏

The Best Of
Intentions

by Helen MacKenzie

Illustration by Siviglia.

F ROM the moment the ring went on my finger, I was clear in my mind how things were going to be. I'd be a really model, modern wife. No slopping round when Craig came home in slippers and an apron. I'd have the kids in bed, the supper timed to perfection, and the house would be immaculate.

I'd be a really model mum, as well. But I'd felt some confusion on

Liathach from Loch Clair, Torridon.

Gordon Henderson.

this score, as the books by baby experts I read while expecting Chloe all said different things.

Mum told me I'd be best to learn as I went along and, if in doubt, to trust my instincts.

The only point I wasn't sure of was whether I should pick Chloe up when she cried at night — the books were terribly divided on the subject. But, once I had a real baby really screeching, and a need for sleep myself, I ditched the advocates of leaving baby alone and nursed her on demand.

I told myself this was a minor blip and there were arguments on my side anyway. Besides, when I was absolutely sure about the rest, why worry if I had one little hiccup? I wouldn't compromise elsewhere.

Of course, the dummy wasn't anything to do with me. I'd set my mind against one from the start. I didn't buy one. Never even looked at one. But then I found one in Chloe's rosebud mouth the first time that Craig's mother babysat for us.

Autumn In Torridon

HERE, as the year grows old,
  Hues of autumn blend;
Traces of yellow-gold
  Signal summer's end.

Rock face and terraced height
  Soar to their summits proud,
Mauve in the mellow light,
  Brushed by a wisp of cloud.

Birches with golden hair
  Dance by the foaming stream;
Berries for winter fare
  Deep in the forest gleam.

Soon, spinning leaves will fall,
  Wither and lose their glow;
Mountains, remote and tall,
  Brood amid wastes of snow.

Now, with her gold and reds,
  Though winter's close at hand,
Autumn her magic spreads
  Over this lovely land.
            — *Brenda G. Macrow.*

She reassured me it was a brilliant comfort and did no harm at all. In fact, it distracted babies from sucking their thumbs. Her four handsome sons had positively thrived on theirs.

I'd wean my daughter off it soon enough, I thought. Besides, it wouldn't do the harm to Chloe that sweets could.

Sweets were probably top of my agenda as she grew a little older. What Chloe never had, she'd never miss, I figured, so if I simply didn't let them slip into her daily life, if I could ration them to once a week, say Saturday . . .

I warned Craig's mother of the ban. My mother, too. I didn't want the doting but well-meaning grannies sabotaging policy. But my plan didn't quite work. Well, *you* try pushing a trolley round a supermarket with confectionery clearly and tantalisingly displayed at toddler level. So much for banning sweets . . .

So much for my determination not to yield to bribery because, as soon as Chloe twigged the supermarket ploy, she realised she could adapt it in all sorts of ways.

And the grannies didn't help. Chloe only had to point to an expensive dress and bang went any hope I had of supermarket fashions! And Craig was useless as an ally. He worshipped Chloe and he couldn't see the harm in spoiling her, especially as we weren't paying . . . I didn't stand a chance.

Except regarding television. I definitely won hands down on that. Chloe's TV watching was strictly rationed. And I wouldn't tolerate the dreadful business of the must-have TV spin-off toys each Christmas. I was extremely proud I didn't buckle under Chloe's pleading and her blackmail, although it wasn't easy. I had to have an iron-clad excuse — like Santa had run out of stock.

This was a problem for me, since I'd set my face against the whole idea of Father Christmas. I guess it's nice enough to start with, but given that it ends in tears of disillusionment . . .

The grannies were appalled at the suggestion — and Craig had already bought a Santa suit for Chloe's first Christmas. So I gave up on that idea.

I HAD soon declared a ban on any other fantasies — excluding *printed* fairy tales, that is. I wanted Chloe to become as keen a reader as I was. What concerned me more as the years wore on was trying to enforce a lights-out time. I had succeeded admirably in my prime objective — Chloe was addicted to books — but she was only seven and I didn't want her sitting up till late each night.

I know she still does now she's eight. I see the chink of light beneath her bedroom door. It steadily defies my curfew, falls across the landing . . . And across the slippers that I vowed I'd never wear. But they are so cosy while I am waiting for her to fall asleep.

She told me she was going to stay up and watch for the tooth fairy and now I'm yawning as I wait for my chance to steal into her room. I'm shattered — all I want is to crawl downstairs and slump on to the sofa, tuck the dressing-gown I find surprisingly to be my style these days around my feet, and cuddle up to Craig.

"If only Chloe didn't have this 'thing' about the dentist," I murmur later, as I lay my head against Craig's shoulder.

He drops a kiss into my hair.

"I bet you anything she puts it on. She's playing you for sympathy. And for the fifty pence."

I yawn, too tired to argue. It's such a hard life, acting as the tooth fairy. I know I swore I would never indulge in that particularly silly myth, but how can I be sure that Chloe hasn't got a phobia about the dentist that isn't eased by looking forward to the magic compensation? She might develop a complex later in her life. I couldn't risk that, could I? Now and then a mother has to swallow hard and compromise.

But I'll be firmer when she's older. I'm quite determined that I will. There'll be no nonsense then. Just wait and see . . .! ❏

T HE doorbell rang insistently, cutting through the sound of the rain that pulsated against the windows.

"Just what I don't need," Janice grumbled as she looked through the peephole and opened the door. It was bad enough that Geoffrey was out of town on this, of all days.

"Good morning, dear." Her mother, an umbrella in one hand and carrier bag in the other, swept into the hall and went straight through to the kitchen.

Janice followed her. Her mother sounded positively chirpy and that made Janice even more irritable.

"What are you doing here, Mum?"

"I can't stay," her mother said, as if Janice had just offered her a cup of tea. "I'm on my way to my garden club meeting, but I thought

by Kathleen Quinn

Illustration by Mike Heslop.

Rising To The Occasion

Overnight Snowfall

SUCH silence here!
The brooding mountains white
Loom in the pallid light.
The trees are bare,
No hint of green on the birch or rowan fine
Only the spruce and pine
Stand proud in frosty air.

Glen Strae, near Dalmally, Argyll.

I'd drop this off first." She put the bags on the kitchen counter.

Janice eyed them suspiciously.

"I have groceries, Mum. I'm perfectly capable of shopping for myself."

"I know, dear. But today's the day the board meets, isn't it?"

Janice nodded.

"Well, I know you took a vacation day so as not to be there when they make the announcement." She shook her head as she looked out the window. "Wouldn't you know you'd have rain?"

meadows cold and sere,
ᴉe snow-capped stacks like Alpine chalets
seem,
ᴉd all is white and still,
ntil the sun, with sudden, blinding beam,
ghts up the distant hill
ᴉd spreads its radiance on the glens below,
:attering diamonds on the virgin snow!
— *Brenda G. Macrow.*

Janice followed her mother's gaze glumly.

"I had planned on doing some cycling today — or at least some work in the garden."

"I know, dear. But with this rain . . . Anyway, bread would be better than cycling or gardening. I thought you might not have all the ingredients for baking it. So —"

"Baking bread? I don't bake bread. I buy bread from the bakery on the next road. You know that." Janice's voice was sharp.

Her mother ignored her and emptied the bags on to the counter.

"I've included a few recipes and some loaf pans. I think everything's here. I even included some poppy seeds in case you want to —"

"I just said I don't bake bread. You do, but I don't." Janice was growing angry.

"I know, dear, but I think you might want to try it today. It always got me through the worst days." She kissed her daughter on the cheek and headed back out the door. "It does help. Honestly."

JANICE closed the door with a bang.

"That woman drives me crazy," she muttered.

Her mother would never understand that *she* had chosen a different route in life. A laptop computer and a briefcase were her chosen tools, not an apron and a measuring cup. She certainly had no interest in following in her mother's footsteps.

Once her mother was gone, Janice put on some music.

Then she fixed a cup of tea and carried it into the living-room. Sitting down in her bentwood rocking chair, she picked up a book which she'd begun over the weekend.

"Now *this* is how *I* spend a rainy day," she said to herself.

She read the same page four times before realising that she couldn't concentrate well enough to read.

Putting the book down, Janice finished sipping her tea. She looked at her watch, but only 20 minutes had passed since her mother had left. The board meeting was scheduled for two o'clock. She had hours to fill.

Would she get the promotion? She knew she deserved it . . . she knew she could handle the added responsibility . . . But she also knew that her age was against her.

They'd never had a vice-president under thirty before.

"This is ridiculous."

She walked back into the kitchen, pointedly ignoring the bread-making equipment, and reached under the sink for her cleaning supplies. It only took her an hour to make the house sparkle — she had done a thorough spring cleaning just a few weeks earlier.

Putting the bucket and soap back under the sink, Janice looked out of the window again. It was no longer pouring — it was bucketing — and the wind had picked up. She turned round and looked at the bags her mother had left.

"I give up." She shrugged and began reading the recipe.

As she measured the flour and emptied it into the bowl, Janice thought about her mother's comment on "the worst days".

She had always assumed that her mother had baked just to show off her domestic skills. But now that she thought about it, her mother *had* baked with a vengeance during troubled times.

Although she had been only six at the time, Janice still had vivid memories of that August afternoon when her mother had come home from hospital after an overnight stay. Her eyes were red from crying, she could tell, but no-one would explain what had happened.

Janice had overheard her father and Aunt Celia talking about her mother losing a baby. At the time, she had wondered how anyone could "lose" a baby.

And they didn't even have any babies to lose. There was just Janice and Mum and Dad.

Ignoring the protests of the other adults, her mother had walked into the kitchen and started assembling baking ingredients and laying out her big baking bowl.

While sitting at the kitchen table, drawing some pictures with her new crayons, Janice had watched her mother mix the ingredients and flour the worktop. She had sat transfixed as her mother began to knead as if nothing in the world was so important.

She had been puzzled by her mother's uncharacteristic silence.

Later, after playing outside with some of the neighbourhood children, Janice had returned to the kitchen. Her mother was tenderly forming tiny rolls, gently stroking them into the desired shapes, while tears streamed down her face.

As Janice began to knead her dough, she recalled another of those "worst days".

She was fourteen and her grandfather had had his first heart attack. They'd received the call early on a Saturday morning.

"Don't come yet," her grandmother had said. "Celia's on her way, but she only has fifty miles to drive. We'll phone you as soon as we know anything. If . . ." Her voice broke. "If he gets any worse, then you'll want to come."

Her mother had moved to the kitchen, as if in a fog, to begin making bread, ignoring the fact that no-one had even had breakfast yet.

Janice remembered how her mother had kneaded that dough almost violently, pounding it, flipping it over and pounding it some more. She had finally stopped to let it rise, then kneaded it again, even more fiercely.

It wasn't until the second phone call had come — the one with the good news — that she had shaped the dough into loaves.

JANICE covered her dough with a tea towel and made herself another cup of tea. She returned to her rocking chair, thinking about other bread-baking moments. None were so dramatic yet each seemed significant.

There was the time her father had lost his bid on a major contract. And the day Janice had come home from school, sobbing, because some of the other children had made fun of her new haircut.

With a pang of regret, she suddenly recalled the night before she left for university, when her mother had tried to help her pack but Janice had rebuffed her. Although it was already ten o'clock, her mother had begun baking bread.

At the time, Janice had thought scornfully that *her* life would be more fulfilling than her mother's. No-one would ever chain *her* to a kitchen.

Her life *was* fulfilling, she thought as she worked. As she shaped the dough into loaves and set them in the pans, again covering them with the damp tea towel, she realised how gracefully her mother had moved through the difficult times.

And selflessly, Janice thought, with another twinge of guilt.

By the time Janice put the raised loaves into the oven, she was feeling relaxed and confident.

Being considered for the position of vice-president was an honour, but she knew that even if she didn't get the promotion this time, she would get it within the next few years.

She set the timer on the cooker, returned to her rocker, and began reading.

Just as the buzzer rang, so did the phone. She carefully removed the loaves, set them to cool, and picked up the receiver.

"Hello?"

She listened to her caller, and began grinning.

"Thank you so much for phoning, Mr Taylor. I'll see you in the morning."

She set the phone down and then picked it up again and dialled.

"Mum? I have some good news. The bread turned out perfectly. It looks almost as good as yours, but I haven't tasted it yet.

"Oh, and I got the promotion." She paused. "Mum? Thank you. For everything." ❏

NOT enough room to swing a cat, Jenny thought as she sat at the small kitchen table, squashed between the washing machine and the stack of bright yellow vegetable baskets Jim had fixed on the wall.

Compact. That's how an estate agent would describe it. But, in truth, it was just *too small*. With a weary sigh, Jenny surveyed the room, slowly and carefully, in a way she hadn't done for years. It wasn't that she didn't like her kitchen. It had been the scene of many happy family occasions.

It was just that . . . well . . . suddenly everywhere she turned there seemed to be more and more clutter and less and less room. And the problem was only going to get worse.

The far wall was plastered with children's paintings. They fought for space next to the deep recessed window overflowing with twisted geranium stems and starbursts of Christmas cacti.

Kirsty's bright daubs from playgroup glowed with smiling egg-shaped faces, while dogs with four legs all in a row trotted across the squares of white paper.

Richard's more sophisticated paintings were of the local castle he'd visited with his school class.

Jenny's gaze travelled up from the art display to the ceiling.

Damp sheets were folded over the ancient pulley above her head. Catching sight of them steaming away in the heat of the old stove, she was suddenly aware of the sound of rain outside. It was a grey day, so dull and depressing.

A tumble dryer, that's what she needed. Small hope of that, though, in this already overcrowded room.

It was no good. They'd have to think seriously about moving to a bigger

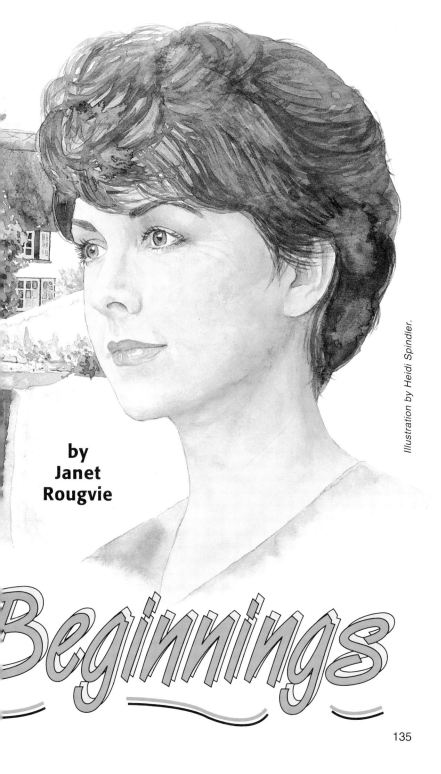

Illustration by Heidi Spindler.

**by
Janet
Rougvie**

Beginnings

house. But Jenny knew that would break Jim's heart and, although she wasn't in the mood for admitting it, probably her own.

They'd bought the cottage eight years earlier, just after their engagement. It had been love at first sight. Who cared if the back wall tended to get damp in the winter, or if it wasn't exactly on a direct bus route?

They'd spotted the *for sale* sign whilst cycling through the village on a sunny Sunday afternoon.

The house had seemed to beckon to them in the June sunshine, and they'd been unable to resist stopping for a rest and taking a closer look.

The cottage had been empty for some time, and an over-adventurous clematis almost covered the top of the cobweb-clad front door.

JIM had propped the garden gate open with the wheel of his bike, and together they'd picked their way up the weedy path, side-stepping the outstretched arms of rose bushes bursting with buds on either side of them.

The garden was enclosed by a thick stone wall and fringed with a mass of sprouting bushes and flower-laden shrubs which intertwined amicably, competing for the sunshine.

Jim had slipped his arms around Jenny and, watched only by the bees buzzing lazily from blossom to scented blossom, they'd celebrated their find with a long kiss. The place radiated happiness and love, and they knew without a shadow of a doubt this was the home for them.

"It's magical," Jim had said as they'd tip-toed cautiously around to the rear of the cottage, reluctant to break the spell. They'd passed the old broken-down shed, leaning drunkenly against the kitchen wall, with its slipped tiles covered in moss, and emerged into the tangled wilderness beyond.

"This is one wonderful garden," he'd whispered in Jenny's ear. "Just perfect for children."

Jenny had looked up at him and smiled at his rapt expression. They'd talked about starting a family as soon as they were married. As one of a large, chaotic brood himself, Jim's idea of heaven was a house full of non-stop laughter and dirty football boots.

Jenny had almost been able to hear the voices of their hoped-for offspring resounding from tree to tree in this lovely place.

The cottage wasn't big, but there was more than enough space for the two of them. Within six months, Jim had tamed the garden and, as soon as Jenny knew there was to be an addition to the family, he began to build a tree house.

"It'll be years before he can climb up there," Jenny had joked.

"She!" her husband had corrected, with raised eyebrows and mock disapproval. "A daughter first, please. Then a son . . . and then maybe another daughter. And perhaps another little boy after that . . ."

She'd swept her arms around his neck and stopped his words with a kiss.

A CENTURY OF CHANGE

All Change!

THERE was outrage and confusion in many banks and shops when, on February 15, 1971, Britain converted to decimal currency. It was a change that had been resisted for years, with bankers and the Chamber of Commerce first calling for decimalisation as far back as 1917!

So we finally said goodbye to shillings, tanners and old pennies. Out went symbols such as 1/- (meaning one old shilling or five new pence) while 'p' replaced 'd' for pence.

Many mourned, in particular, the end of the half-crown (now 12.5 pence), while others found it hard to adjust to the idea of a ten-pence coin, which equalled a florin (the old two shillings).

One of the most common fears was that shopkeepers would use the change to mark up prices and it took a while to get used to the new price tags.

It was, however, very welcome news for foreign tourists as it made life so much easier when changing their holiday money.

• • • • • • • • • 1970 – 1979 • • • • • • • • • •

"Enough! Let's just take things one at a time."

But now, as Jenny sat in the kitchen reminiscing, it all seemed a long time ago. The babies had indeed arrived one at a time and the home they all loved so much had somehow grown smaller and smaller.

As the clock ticked comfortingly on the wall behind her, Jenny finished her careful inspection of the familiar room. Beside her in his carry-cot, baby Neil stirred and snuffled in his sleep and she gazed at her chubby nine-month-old son, with his wisps of golden hair.

She stood up after a moment and moved towards the old mirror hanging behind the kitchen door. Its edge was brown where the silvering had worn away.

A bit like me, Jenny thought wryly. Getting a bit frazzled at the edges. But the face that looked back at Jenny was still a pretty one. Her brown eyes were bright and clear, and her skin fresh. Yet somehow her face looked tense.

She knew things were starting to get on top of her. Struggling with the sudden rush of feelings which flooded through her, she felt the tears begin to prick.

Why did she have to feel like this, she thought angrily to herself. Here she was, with the most beautiful baby sleeping peacefully within arm's length, and two much-loved children to collect within the hour. Her husband was still the man she had fallen in love with. She was so lucky.

Why on earth couldn't she bloom with contentment rather than get depressed about the cottage?

Yet, once, it had seemed so perfect. She remembered cuddling up with Jim by the big log fire in the sitting-room on their first wedding anniversary . . . She'd pulled the thick russet curtains snugly across the stone window seat to shut out the dark, and they'd slowly shared a bottle of champagne.

The twilight had drained away to darkness and, determined not to let anything spoil their firelit scene, they'd brought every candle they had in the house into the room. It had been so romantic.

She cast a glance towards the sitting-room doorway. Now there was a pram there, as well as a playpen, and baby clothes drying around the well-guarded fire. A lit candle would be nothing more than a fire hazard nowadays, and she'd be more likely to find a baby's bottle than a champagne glass!

THE ringing phone cut into her thoughts and Jenny stretched awkwardly backwards to lift the receiver from the wall. Trying not to let her voice sound too wobbly, she swallowed hard and forced a bright "hello". Oblivious to her hesitant opening, an excited voice burst over the phone line.

"Jen? Jenny, I want you to sit down right now and pour yourself a large brandy."

Jenny recognised Linda's voice. Linda lived nearby with her husband, Graham, and the two women had first met long ago at school. What had started as a childhood friendship had developed into a deep affection between them — marred only by Jenny's secret sense of guilt.

Whilst she and Jim seemed to accumulate offspring as easily as hens lay eggs, Linda and Graham had tried desperately to start a family.

Jenny felt rather ashamed. She'd been feeling sorry for herself because her life and home seemed to have been taken over by children and motherhood. But what, she wondered, would her best friend give to be in the same situation? Worse, though — she knew she'd eventually have to break her own news to Linda — the news she was dreading telling her.

The news that Jenny realised was the real cause of her sitting feeling so down in her little kitchen . . .

With a calmness which she was far from feeling, Jenny forced a half laugh into the phone.

"A brandy? At this time of the day?"

"You'll need one when you hear — and you're the first we're telling," came the excited reply.

"We've done it at last, Jen. I can hardly believe it's true, but it is. I'm expecting!"

The tension that had built up in Jenny during the last month suddenly seemed to leave her and she felt full of happiness for her friend. And everything seemed back in perspective — albeit a rather queasy one! She knew she'd have a few more weeks yet of feeling down. It had been exactly the same with Richard, Kirsty and Neil.

But pregnancies being what they are, she also knew that she would wake one morning feeling wonderful again. The hormone fairy would have come in the night!

"Oh, Linda!" The words caught in Jenny's throat. "I can't tell you how happy I am. And I've been sitting here all morning having a good weep — even thinking about suggesting to Jim we sell the cottage and get somewhere with more room.

"Can you imagine what the children would say about losing the garden and the tree-house?"

"A good weep?" The concern was immediate in Linda's reply. "What on earth's the matter? Here's me so full of myself, I hadn't a clue there was anything wrong."

"But there isn't." Jenny laughed into the phone — a real laugh this time, full of warmth and contentment.

"I didn't know how to tell you before, but you're not the only one with a surprise. Mine will be number four, rather than number one, but we're still delighted.

"It's just that I always feel rotten for the first three months or so — then it passes like magic. But your news has already worked wonders."

"Jenny —" Linda's voice was suddenly hesitant "— this was meant to be a surprise. But I know Graham has been helping your Jim with some plans for the cottage. There's plenty of space for an extension!"

A whoop of pleasure came from the other end of the phone.

"Oh, Linda — I knew he was up to something." Jenny was thrilled.

"We must get together," Linda was saying. "Graham and I will come round tonight. We've got so much to talk about. I'll help you put the kids to bed, then we'll have that glass of brandy by the fire. Well, the men can — we'd better stick to orange juice!"

"Great," Jenny said. "Oh, Linda, you've made me so happy!" With a quiet sigh, Jenny ran her hand over her tummy, imagining the tiny new life inside. It was the perfect time for great new beginnings . . . and suddenly she felt the luckiest woman in the world! ❏

JOE stood in front of the dressing-table mirror, straightening his tie and slicking down his already immaculate hair.

He didn't hear Bryony come up behind him. Then soft arms came round his neck.

With one hand she pulled the lobe of his ear, a familiar gesture which had lingered from the heady days of first love. He knew there would be a little criticism to follow.

"Joe, please, not that tie. I know Polly gave it to you for Christmas, but don't you think it's more a family-day-out tie than a very-important-meeting-with-the-boss kind?"

Another tie waved in front of his nose.

"And that's your idea of what an up and coming 'secutive — as Polly used to describe me — should wear to impress?"

"Dull, but worthy. I can't even remember where it came from." She

by Judy Chard

Illustration by M. Thorsen.

eyed the dark red tie with a frown.

"Looking at it, probably Aunt Enid."

"So it'll have done the rounds of all the family!"

He smiled as he knotted the tie.

"OK, I give in. I'm sure you know best."

He turned and kissed the end of her attractive nose, glad she had passed it on to their two children instead of his.

"Like the White Rabbit in Alice, 'I'm late, I'm late'!" He ran downstairs.

Polly and her big brother were eating at the breakfast bar. Paul, shovelling in porridge as if he was eating for Britain, didn't look like the family brainbox. You'd never know he was headed for university to be a biochemist.

Then there was Polly. Joe gazed at her fondly — the apple of his eye. Oh, at times he could murder them both — they were ordinary teenagers, for which both he and Bryony were thankful.

But Polly was special to him. She'd inherited his talent for worrying,

sion Time

especially where any living thing was concerned. She was a clever artist, and Joe already knew, though she said she didn't, what her career was likely to be.

He was determined neither of them would be pushed into anything they did not enjoy. He loved his own job, dealing with people, and that

was why his sales graph showed consistent success.

It was a long time now since he'd sold his first car. Bryony had just qualified as a stylist at the hair salon then. Two teenagers later, she was back at work there, and usually dropped off the kids at school en route.

Today was different — Joe was meeting the chairman, Ted Gibbons, to be interviewed for a seat on the board. Sales Director! He and Alan Carter were the only candidates.

Sometimes Joe felt his chances were slim — Alan had been to public school; his wife was well in with a lot of influential people in

ANNE and I went to church on a bright spring morning. There was a hope of summer in the air and a slight breeze came in off the sea.

Sunday lunch was light. We have, when there are just the two of us, cut out the roast beef and Yorkshire pudding plus all the trimmings.

Today, there was no soup; instead homemade pâté on a piece of toast, then a homemade lasagne with a side salad. (I was allowed to make the salad.)

After washing up, I was at the back door looking across the yard.

"Anne, come here a minute."

When she joined me, I pointed to two swallows trying to keep their balance on our telephone wire. The were the first arrivals of the season.

"Now for trouble," Anne said.

They're not her favourite bird, bu I enjoy them about the place. They' often better guides to the weather

Feathere

by John Taylor

the town . . . her father had been mayor.

Sitting down at his place, he saw a pink envelope propped against the milk jug. Polly never missed an opportunity to find just the right card for any occasion.

He opened it. The card showed a racehorse about to take an enormous jump, with a jockey in bright silks on its back.

"Let no obstacle be in your way in life's Grand National," said the wording — Polly going over the top as usual!

He went over and hugged her.

"That is definitely exactly what I needed to boost my confidence, pet. I can't possibly fail now!" He kissed the end of her nose, so like Bryony's.

riends

an the men at the Met Office!
Anne and I once had a terrible
w over these beautiful birds.
It was the end of May, maybe 20
ars ago, when Anne noticed that a
ir had built their nest in the top
rner of the spare bedroom
ndow. I was instructed to bring a
lder and knock the nest down.
I knew why — once the eggs are
tched and the birds fly in and out
th food for their young, they make
errible mess with their droppings.
I took the ladder, climbed up and
ind the nest already had three eggs
it. I refused to do the necessary
molition.
We argued — and I won. But the
ςs soon hatched and I cleared up
ce the nest was empty.

FTER lunch, we'd agreed to go
for a walk up to the top land
d down by the burn.
We'd gone through the gate and
o a field we used to plough but
ve now put down to grass, when a

he Farmer And His Wife

whirl of wings sprang up from under
our very feet. It was a brace of
partridge.
We were both delighted!
Until three years ago, there was
always a brace to be found in a
certain area near an old hedge on the
Riggin. We thought our couple had
come to an untimely end, but here
they were, back with us again.
It put a new spring into our step as
we made the top land and rested
against the big rock there, looking
out to May Island.
Then we walked down to the burn
and marvelled at the beauty of the
trees, with such bright greeny yellow
leaves. What a variety of different
shapes and sizes of both leaves and
trees.
We stood looking up at a big old
sycamore in both leaf and flower.
The humming from the thousands
of bees in that tree was unbelievable.
Where had they come from? Anne
and I couldn't think where the
nearest hives were.
Looking down at the burn, we saw
our two dipper friends, which meant
they hadn't started to build their nest
yet.
We went back to the Riggin
delighted. We'd had a very enjoyable
afternoon.

No time to read the paper, which stood neatly folded by his place.
He seldom did, anyway. What the kids and Bryony had to say was
usually much more interesting than all the local headlines.
"Have some honey with that, Dad."
Quickly he swallowed his porridge, laced with honey, a hangover
from Polly's interest in how much good bees did you.

HE got to his feet, and as he did so, a vision appeared in the
hall with a large, aggrieved-looking ginger cat in her arms.
"Someone shut Montgomery in the downstairs loo again.
He hates it in there! It only makes him even more crochety with
Winston when he gets out."

"Nanny Dot, you look drop-dead gorgeous," Polly said, pouring oil on troubled waters.

Joe eyed his mum fondly. You never knew with Dot. Sometimes she liked to play at being a storybook grandmother in classic clothes with a manner to match. At other times — and today was obviously one of those — she turned into Supergran.

Today Supergran was in a bright pink leisure suit and was beaming fondly at her granddaughter.

"Thank you, my blossom. You look pretty good yourself — school uniform isn't half as grotty as when I was young."

"School uniform didn't exist at Godwall Infants!" Joe laughed down at his mother, who just about reached his shoulder, pecked her cheek and made quickly for the hall before she could cover his suit in ginger hairs.

"You haven't forgotten it's my morning for water aerobics, have you, son?"

Joe had. And he also realised he was standing in his socks. Paul had been polishing his shoes studiously, making them gleam.

"Good grief! I had. Why not come to the office with me? Then you can have a taxi the rest of the way to the pool."

"Lift up your foot, Dad." Paul pulled a shoe on to one of his father's feet and tied the laces.

Joe looked down at his son's shining hair, remembering how recently it had been him doing that for Paul.

"No call for a taxi, Joe. I think I can manage to stagger round to the leisure centre. But I would like a lift later, because it's bingo this afternoon and after aerobics I'll be stiff as a crow.

"That Annabel doesn't half put us through our paces! Nick Turner said he'd put his back out last week, but it suddenly went back in again after she'd given him a massage, cheeky monkey."

NANNY Dot had her rooms at the top of the house where she could entertain her friends, and have her own telly and music. Naturally, things didn't always run entirely smoothly.

Montgomery was the main snag to living with Nanny Dot. The consequent dead mice and birds upset both Polly and Bryony, the latter more because of the state of her kitchen floor, where he invariably dropped them.

Dot had named the cat Montgomery after the general, and Polly called the guide dog puppy she was walking Winston, hoping to bring some measure of friendship between the two. It hadn't worked.

Winston was a typical Labrador, friendly to a fault and into everything, but completely devoid of the responsibility he'd need to be a guide dog. Polly, secretly relieved, had been happy to buy him and welcome him home for good.

144

Seven mouths to feed! This place on the board would mean not only promotion, but a welcome increase in salary.

The first thing he and Bryony had in mind was to build Nanny Dot a self-contained extension, with access to the main house . . .

At last, Joe had the car out in the drive. Dot settled in the passenger seat and turned the radio on.

"Nice to have a CD player in here. You've got good speakers, Joe."

He tried to hide his amusement. She was a modern granny all right — Dotty by name and Dotty by nature.

The early morning traffic was solid. As they waited at a crossing, Dot laid a hand on his knee.

"Tell me about this interview, son. It means a lot to you, doesn't it?"

For a moment, he covered her hand with his own, and all at once some of the tension which had been building up inside him eased.

"It's a seat on the board, Ma. The job's between the sales manager from Manchester and me. Old man Gibbons is coming to interview me today after he's seen Alan Carter."

As they moved off again, he told her how he felt about Alan, his education and well-connected wife.

"Rubbish!" It was a big explosion for such a tiny person. "From all I hear, you're good at your job. Always bright, you were, like your dad, God rest his soul."

Joe shook his head, his eyes on the road.

"Ted Gibbons is a hard nut. You wouldn't think he had half a pint of the milk of human kindness in him."

"You make him sound like a coconut!" His mother laughed.

"When Bryony and I went to dinner with him, Alan and his wife were there. They didn't half make us feel like a couple of hicks from the sticks."

Dot was thoughtful.

"What's Ted's wife like?"

"Oh, a super lady. She made us feel quite at ease, but the talk after dinner was a bit above our heads — opera, books, plays we'd never heard of . . ."

The car glided effortlessly up the hill to the showroom.

"Remember the hill I had to climb to school? Always an east wind biting my bare knees. There was a big house at the top, with iron gates and neat flowerbeds, rather like where Ted Gibbons lives."

"That was the place where I worked as a cleaner." Dot nodded. "They was hard days, luv, but we had some laughs. And I had you and Sylvia, Jane and Jack. It wasn't easy, bringing up four kids with your dad gone, but worth every minute. I'm proud of you all."

Oh, those days of hand-me-down clothes, shrunken woollies, bread and dripping, fish and chips . . . all the sacrifices he knew Dot had made . . .

"It's you I have to thank for where we all are," he said gruffly. "And I know that the others would say the same, Ma."

"Get a life!" she exploded, making Joe laugh so much he nearly bowled over an old lady.

At the showroom, he asked again if she'd like a taxi. Her only reply was a snort of derision and the familiar thumbs up sign, to wish him luck, an echo from the past when exams loomed.

For a moment, he stood watching the slim, upright figure as she strode along the pavement. There were more eyes than his on the happy woman in the pink suit.

IN the office, Daphne greeted him with her usual warm smile. She was probably as anxious as he was that he should get the job — it would add to her prestige as well, if that meant anything.

"I think it might be an idea if you brought the coffee as soon as Mr Gibbons arrives, please, Daph. I expect the motorway is almost at a standstill as usual." He paused. "I wonder if . . ."

But she was ahead of him.

"I hope I did right, Mr Fenton. I bought a bottle of whisky . . . the brand the chairman likes."

She waited with a touch of apprehension for his approval.

"You did well, lass. Leave it on the side there. If the interview goes near lunch time, perhaps . . ."

She nodded and smiled.

"Good luck, Mr Fenton."

He riffled through the post, marking one or two letters to remind himself of how to reply, but he couldn't settle.

Ted Gibbons was usually punctual . . .

He went over to the window, looking across the showroom complex.

Yes, he'd come a long way since those backstreet days he'd been talking to Mum about. He'd had no helping hand but Ma . . . and she'd kept him studying when other boys were kicking cans round the alleyways, dating, dancing.

Here was Ted's Rolls now. The chauffeur got out and opened the

Arbroath, Angus

IN 1599 the fishing port of Arbroath became a Royal Burgh, but it was in 1320 that history was made here when the Declaration Of Arbroath was signed in the Abbey.

Today tourists can still see the ruins of Arbroath Abbey and wander round the small harbour, popping in to one of the fishmongers to buy a local delicacy — Arbroath Smokies. It's not surprising that these delicious smoked haddock are popular with visitors and locals alike.

ARBROATH, ANGUS : J CAMPBELL KERR

door, and Ted alighted, smoking the usual cigar.

Joe went back to his desk and shuffled his papers; not too neat, not too chaotic.

Would he be able to tell from the expression on Ted's face how Alan's interview had gone? He felt the sweat run down between his shoulder blades.

THE door opened wide and Ted came in, laughing at Daphne over his shoulder.

"Coffee soon as you like, lass. It's a long way down from Manchester.

"Well, Joe, lad, h'are ya?"

Ted's usual hearty handshake.

Joe pulled out the armchair by the coffee table, making small talk, asking how Mrs Gibbons was, had they enjoyed their holiday in the Maldives — was it the Maldives? He wasn't too sure. He was beginning to feel an odd kind of detachment, as if he were watching the scene outside himself.

Ted made appropriate answers, settled himself, straightened one trouser leg and crossed his ankles. It was obvious he was enjoying this.

"Well, Joe — I see the sales are behaving themselves. What is your opinion of the new model they're sending us?"

The new small car in the showroom had quite an outstanding personality.

What would Alan have said, though? Joe knew he'd criticised the time for the launch; Alan thought it would have been better at Easter, catch the summer buyers . . .

He hesitated a moment, just as Daphne gave a discreet knock and came in with the coffee.

As she turned to go, he opened his mouth to reply, and looked across at Ted.

The chairman was staring, open mouthed himself, beyond Daphne to the outer office. Standing there was a vision in a pink leisure suit.

For a moment he closed his eyes. Please God, a miracle, an earthquake, anything, he thought.

But no — here came Ma.

He looked at her round cheerful face, remembered their talk in the car, and was ashamed of himself.

He went towards her, holding out his hands.

"Hello, son. Trouble with 't'pool — too much chlorine in the water. Why they have to fiddle around with the Lord's good clean water, heaven knows."

"Just in time for coffee, Ma!" He put his arm round her as Daphne quietly brought in a third cup. After all, Ma was a sight more important than any job.

At The Fair

THE fair upon the common
Was such a lovely sight;
Skelter slides and pony rides —
All was sheer delight.

Coconut shies and hoop-la stalls —
We're hoping to win a prize.
Bright attractions of the fair
Bring joy to childish eyes.

Swinging boats and a roundabout,
And towering Ferris wheel.
Long tunnels on the ghost train
Which make us laugh and squeal.

A penny whistle, candy-floss,
A funny-faced balloon —
All pleasures of the fairground
That ended all too soon!
— *Dorothy M. Loughran.*

Ted had put his cigar in the ashtray before he stood up.

Dot held out her hand, smiling up at him with clear blue eyes.

"May I introduce my mother? Mr Gibbons, Ma."

"Pleased to meet you, I'm sure."

For a moment, Ted hesitated and Joe tightened his hold on his mother's shoulders.

"It isn't? It can't be . . ." Ted came closer. "I don't believe it! Little Dotty Potter from Godwall Infants. You sat in front of me and I put your pigtails down the inkwell! I didn't half get a walloping from old man Thomas."

Ma peered at the chairman.

"Well, I never. Giglamp Gibbons! We always called you that on account of those great specs . . ." She giggled. "Fancy you working with my Joe."

Working *with* him? Joe's heart missed a beat, something it was getting used to. You could hardly say the chairman worked *with* one of

149

the sales managers.

Evidently Ted hadn't heard what Dot said, or perhaps he had got some milk of human kindness, after all. Because the chairman was showing Ma to a chair.

"Remember Spotty Muldoon, and Dick Franks? Put a frog in Thomas's desk. Spotty's some bigwig in Brussels now . . ."

"Whatever happened to old man Thomas?" Dot wondered aloud.

"Dead, m'dear. The drink, I heard . . . sad . . . Well, I'm blessed. So you're Joe's mum! He's a lucky lad. I had no idea."

He poured another cup of coffee, passing it to Dot.

"Haven't you done well, as the man said?" she remarked.

"He is the boss," Joe said quietly, and she grinned.

"I could see that from the cigar!" She laughed at Ted. Laughed! At the chairman!

I T"S grand to see you, Dot." Ted was sitting back in his chair, enjoying himself. "You haven't changed a bit. I'd have known you anywhere. And your boy's done well for himself. I like to see a young chap showing consideration for his ma . . . something they don't teach at these high-falutin' academies!"

He winked at Joe. The north-country tones were back in his voice as he talked to Dot.

Then he glanced at his watch.

"Tell you what, Dot, I've got a bit of business to talk over with Joe. How would you like to go over to the Roller, talk to Frank? He drives me around — he went to Godwall Infants as well; after us, though, he's still a youngster." Ted paused.

"Then we three could go out for a slap-up lunch, to celebrate your boy joining the board."

Joe's mouth was open again. He was certain he would wake up in a moment, and find all this was a dream.

Ma's eyes were shining — she was choking back tears, he could see, but she wouldn't say anything about her pride in him. That wasn't Ma's way.

"Just one snag, Ted. My mate Junie and I were going to bingo this afternoon. I don't like to let her down."

Ted rubbed his hands.

"No need to disappoint the good lady. Mind, she may care for a break from bingo. A little country drive and a spot of tea at a pleasant hostelry I know? I believe we can safely leave the business here in the new director's hands for an hour or two this afternoon."

He opened the door for Dot, and raised one of the work-worn hands to his lips.

She played up to him, of course. Then she looked over Ted's shoulder to Joe and gave her thumbs-up sign.

All was well in Joe's world. ❏

Something In Common

by
**Suzanne
Thorpe**

Illustration by M. Thorsen.

"Y OU *have*
remembered
Maddie's
bringing
Josh home tonight
to meet us?" Kate
said as Tom settled
into his recliner
chair with the
evening newspaper.

"Josh? But I
thought Martin was the
love of her life."

Kate sighed and
nodded him to lean
forward as she went
round plumping up
cushions.

"Don't you ever
notice anything?
Martin's history and
has been for months
now."

Tom glanced up.

"Pity. He seemed a
nice young man. A bit
quiet . . . but he liked
golf."

Kate smiled at the
reminder of the
smartly-dressed young

151

man Maddie had brought home, slightly spotty and with all the personality of a poached egg.

"Maddie may be our only daughter, but she's eighteen and we can't choose her boyfriends for her."

Tom settled into the recliner.

"Wouldn't dream of it . . ." he murmured as Kate went back to her cushion-plumping.

Just then, they heard two excited voices in the hall.

Maddie and Josh hesitated nervously in the sitting-room doorway.

Kate gave them a warm smile, easing the tension and they grinned back. She couldn't help noticing Josh had warm brown eyes and an open face. He looked as if he laughed a lot . . . at least when he wasn't meeting his girlfriend's parents for the first time!

Tom just stared at the young man with the ponytail and torn denim jeans. His trainers, too, were worn and shabby.

"Sit down, Josh, and I'll make some tea," Kate began briskly. "What er . . . what did Maddie say you were studying at college?"

"Economics," Josh replied.

There was a strained silence and then Tom cleared his throat.

"So . . . do you like golf?" he asked unashamedly.

* * * *

"You didn't like him, did you?" Maddie asked unsteadily once Josh had left.

Tom struggled for an answer.

"I didn't say anything, love," he said defensively.

"Exactly! You hardly said two words to him all evening!"

And with that rather tearful outburst, Maddie rushed out, thundering upstairs to her room.

"What's wrong with her?" Tom appealed to Kate.

"She's obviously found the right young man — that's what's *wrong*!" she snapped.

He sat down again, dazed, and wondering if he would ever understand women!

He made a new attempt when Kate came back from the kitchen.

"He's a nice enough lad — I just wasn't expecting him to look like that. I mean, Martin was so smart . . ."

She gave an incredulous laugh.

"Never expected him to look like *what*? I can remember a certain young man meeting my parents for the first time in purple bell-bottoms, red ankle boots, and a pink flowered shirt!"

Tom picked up the paper again and cringed behind it.

"That was different. Your father and I had a lot in common. He grew flowers — and I wore them."

Kate sighed and shook her head.

"Well, I think you should make an effort to like Josh because you do have something in common — Maddie."

O H hello, Josh, come in."
Josh was wearing the same knee-less jeans, but with a different T-shirt which had had the sleeves roughly cut off. But then, as Tom reminded himself, it *was* summer.

"Have we still got that canvas sheet in the garage, Dad?" Maddie asked.

Tom thought for a moment.

"Somewhere . . . yes."

"Can we borrow it then?"

"If you can find it." He shrugged. "What are you going to do — wear it?" he muttered, then felt Kate's well-aimed elbow in his ribs.

"No." Maddie scowled. "We're planning a camping trip —"

Kate and Tom had just taken a pot of tea through to the patio when Maddie and Josh reappeared.

"How long have you had that old motor cycle, Mr Fielding? It's a 'James Captain', isn't it?"

Tom perked up at the mention of the former love of his life, stashed away under camping equipment and boxes.

"Call me Tom," he said, warming to the young man.

"I've had that bike since I was about your age. Not many people would have known what kind it was."

Josh's eyes were shining as he rushed on excitedly.

"Bikes are one of my hobbies. Perhaps we could take a look at this one, just now?"

Maddie frowned and she glanced at Kate for support. But her mother merely sighed and sank back into her chair.

"Have I got an old T-shirt?" Tom asked, looking down at his sky blue golfing sweater.

"No," Kate said, "but I think you will have . . . shortly."

It couldn't go on, Kate had decided. For one thing, Tom was ruining quite a few sports shirts with oily stains she couldn't budge. But, more importantly, his re-kindled interest in bikes was affecting Maddie's relationship with Josh.

He'd hardly spent any time with her that entire week, ending up with Tom in the garage, trying to piece their motor cycle jig-saw back together again.

So Kate had decided on a little repair work of her own. When Josh arrived on the doorstep that evening, she was there to greet him.

She was all set with her rehearsed suggestion that he and Maddie should go out on such a lovely summer's evening when she found she didn't have to.

Josh, it seemed, had already made other plans.

"Will you tell Tom I can't help with the bike this evening?" He paused to smile over Kate's shoulder as Maddie appeared. "Maddie and I have made other plans — I hope he won't be too disappointed," he added anxiously.

Kate smiled broadly.

"Don't worry," she assured Josh, "he won't be . . . I'll see to that."

TOM looked up when Kate walked in to the garage and wiped an oily hand over his brow.

"Where's Josh? We're supposed to be getting these brakes right tonight."

She shook her head and stifled a smile. Years ago, when they were supposed to be dating, she would sit beside him on a groundsheet, lovingly handing spanners to him.

"Josh has something else to do tonight, Tom." Kate paused, feeling her way carefully, not wanting to hurt his feelings.

"When I said you should get to know Josh better, I didn't mean for you to take him over completely!"

He stood up, wiped his hands on an oily rag, and looked worried.

"Did I . . .?"

"No more than you neglected me." Kate shrugged.

Tom looked even more concerned, then slowly broke into a smile, holding out his arms to her.

"Come over here then and let me give you a hug!"

She pulled a face.

"Not until you've had a wash and got rid of that oil!"

He chuckled, casting a longing look at the partly re-assembled motorbike, and then went indoors.

He was hardly in the house when Maddie and Josh turned up, looking like two people bursting with happiness. They had, Maddie told her parents, something to show them . . .

It was parked at the end of the drive — a well-preserved car, resprayed a striking shade of mauve.

"We bought it today," Maddie said, biting her lip as she waited and hoped for her parents' approval. "It's got its MOT and is in really good condition for its age."

"We've been saving up for ages," Josh added. "Every penny!"

Kate cupped a hand over a smile and gazed fondly now at Josh's knee-less jeans and worn trainers.

"So we were wondering whether you'd both like to go out with us for a spin?"

"Love to!" Tom stepped forward, but Kate laid a restraining hand on his arm.

A Right Royal Baby

'M obviously thrilled and delighted," declared an excited Prince of Wales as he left St Mary's Hospital, Paddington, just two hours after the birth of his son and heir on June 21, 1982.

A week later, the name of the baby, who'd weighed in at 7lb 1.5oz, was announced. He was to be christened William Arthur Philip Louis and would be known as Wills.

For Diana, Princess of Wales, who'd been married less than a year and was still ten days short of her twenty-first birthday, the birth must have seemed like the fulfilment of all her dreams. When her second son, Henry Charles Albert David (Harry) was born two years later on September 16, 1984, it seemed that the young family was complete.

Sadly, less happy times were to follow but, throughout all their troubles, one thing was never in doubt — the devotion of the Royal couple to their children.

William has grown into a sensitive, caring young man, while Harry has won everyone over with his sense of fun and his affability. And it won't be long before they grow into real Royal heartbreakers.

Snowdon, Camera Press

• • • • • • • • • 1980–1989 • • • • • • • • •

"Not looking like that, you won't! You'd get oil on their car seats!" she told him warningly.

Tom looked ruefully down at his rather dirty shirt and they all laughed easily together.

And, later, as they all climbed into the "new" car, Tom couldn't help thinking how right he'd been all along. Josh was the perfect partner for his daughter Maddie — no matter what Kate had said about his fashion sense! ❑

Islands In The Sky

LILAC sheen the water shrouds,
  Wavelets lap the shore serene,
Purple isles and purple clouds
  Frame the glory in between.

Birds are silent on the heath,
Petals close on mountain flower,
Nature seems to hold her breath
In this still, enchanted hour.

Yet slow time must forward creep
  Till the flames of sunset die,
Till the night's dark shadows deep
  Drown the islands in the sky.
  — *Brenda G. Macrow.*

J. Winkley.

Loch nan Uamh, Morar.

BZZZZ!" The insistent buzz of the doorbell woke Emily with a start.

"I must have dozed off!" She pushed her spectacles up her nose, struggled to her feet and turned off the television. The bell buzzed again.

"I'm coming, I'm coming," she muttered, unlocking the door. "What's the hurry? Can't you wait . . .? Oh, my!"

Illustration by Barcilon.

Standing on the pavement was a tall, broad-shouldered young man with an enormous grin on his tanned face. His hair was sun-bleached and his blue eyes had fine lines at the corners. He wore a denim jacket and jeans.

"G'day." He paused. "Hello, Auntie Em."

Emily clutched the door frame, hardly able to believe her eyes.

"Matthew?"

"Nowadays everyone calls me Matt," he said, his eyes twinkling.

It must have been nearly ten years since Emily's great-nephew had gone off to Australia.

"Have you got a bed for a weary traveller from Oz?" he asked. "I'm sorry I didn't warn you, but I wanted it to be a surprise."

"It is that! I could have had a heart attack." Emily held the door wide. "Come along in. There's always room for my favourite nephew."

"I'll get my gear."

by Renée Langdon

He turned to the ancient car parked behind him, opened the boot and removed a battered suitcase and holdall.

"Found this my first day back." He patted the old car lovingly. "Remember how I always loved these cars? I'm going to do her up."

In the living-room, he put down his baggage and opened his arms.

"How about a hug, Auntie Em?"

Matthew had always been a loving, tactile little boy. She'd heard those words many times.

He bent down and lifted her off her feet. It was a good feeling — having strong arms around her.

"That's enough of that nonsense," she said briskly as he put her down. She smoothed her hair, and they smiled at each other.

"Now, what about a cup of tea?"

She bustled into the kitchen and filled the kettle.

"Let me do that."

"You will not!" She held the kettle away from him. "This is my kitchen."

"OK!" He held up his hands in mock surrender.

"You can get out the biscuits. The tin is in that cupboard. I suppose

159

you still like custard creams?" She was smiling.

Back in the living-room, she put on another bar of the fire.

"I expect you find it a bit cold after all that sunshine?" she said as they sat down opposite one another.

"It makes a change." He helped himself to a biscuit.

"It's really wonderful to see you," Emily confessed, beaming. "I do enjoy reading your letters. They're so interesting. And now — I can't believe you're really here. You've changed a lot, Matt."

"I should hope so." He grinned. "I was a very young twenty when I took off.

"I've learnt a lot since then — stuff they don't teach at university. But nothing seems to have changed here since I came for holidays . . . except everything seems smaller."

She looked round, seeing it with his eyes. What must he be used to in Australia? She'd never had much money, and had thought herself lucky to be able to buy a place of her own. But he must just see a small, rather shabby house . . .

EMILY had never married. When her only sister, Alice, died, leaving a husband and small daughter, Emily had been largely responsible for young Mary's upbringing.

She and Mary had stayed in close touch, writing regularly, after her niece married and moved away.

Of Mary's three children, Matthew had always been her favourite. His frequent visits to the little house in Ladysmith Street had been exciting events.

"What made you decide to come back for a holiday?" she asked. "And how's your mother — my little Mary? I haven't heard for a while."

Matthew's father had died halfway through his university course and, to his mother's dismay, Matthew had decided to go off to Australia.

Three years later, after Matthew's sisters had married, Mary had gone out to visit him, and there she'd met and married a widower with two grown children.

To everyone's amazement, she'd produced a second son at the age of forty-seven, and was now happily settled with her new family.

"Ma's great," Matt said. "Bill's a good guy, and you should see young Corey! I've got some snaps."

He fished in his holdall, and they spent the afternoon exchanging family news, looking at photographs and reminiscing.

"Now then," Emily said at last. "We must get you something to eat. You must be starving."

"Let me, Aunt Em," Matt immediately offered cheerfully.

He took the mugs out to the kitchen and she heard him opening cupboards and the fridge, seeing what she'd got to eat.

"Why don't I go out and do a bit of shopping for you?" he suggested.

"You don't need to, dear. Alison will be here in a minute."

"Who's Alison?"

"She's . . . Oh! That's her now."

As the doorbell buzzed, Emily got to her feet.

"I'll get it."

She heard his voice in the hall.

"Hi, I'm Matt Carpenter. Come on in — Auntie Em's expecting you."

Alison came in with a bag of groceries and a red haversack. She was twenty-eight, but looked older, with her dark hair scraped back severely, and her clear brown eyes hidden behind her glasses.

"I think I got everything, Miss Cook. And I got you a couple of library books."

She fished them out of her haversack, and Emily took them.

"Bless you, dear," Emily said. "I haven't read either. I shall enjoy these!" She turned to Matthew.

"Alison very kindly does a bit of shopping for me, and, as she works at the library, she's also good enough to keep me in reading material. This is my great-nephew — from Australia. I've told you about Matthew." She watched as Matt and Alison shook hands.

"Alison Moore," the younger woman said, and to Emily, "I'll put these things away for you."

She went off to the kitchen, closely followed by Matt, and Emily heard the murmur of voices.

I don't suppose a pork chop, a couple of carrots and one packet of lasagne will get us far for tea, she thought . . . Then Matt stuck his head round the door.

"I'm just going to the supermarket with Alison," he said. "We're doing tea for you. Back soon."

And Emily heard the front door close.

* * * *

"Have you known Aunt Em long?" Matt asked as he eased his old car out into the street.

"Almost two years. We met at the library," Alison said.

"You must be the friend she keeps referring to in her letters. I don't remember her mentioning your name."

"I was putting books back on the shelves when I noticed her. She looked as if she was going to pass out, so I got a chair and a glass of water . . . it was a very hot day.

"We got talking, and found we lived in the same street. Small world, isn't it? So I offered to take her books home for her. It seemed the least

I could do. She insisted she was OK and could get home on her own."

"That's Auntie Em. Stubborn as a mule."

"When I went round that evening, I stayed for a cup of tea and a biscuit, and we got talking. She always gets the custard creams for me now. She . . ."

Matt laughed.

"There! And I thought she must have second sight and she'd got them for me. They're my favourites, too."

ALISON couldn't help smiling. Miss Cook's nephew had an attractive laugh. In fact, he was very attractive altogether. She felt a warmth, sitting here with him. He made her want to smile all the time.

"We both love books, you see," she went on. "And she's always so interested in everything. She asks about my friends, and work . . ."

"Boyfriends?"

"Not lately," she said coolly, and Matt winced. "And, of course, she's always talking about you. She reads me your letters."

"Does she get out much? She really looks a lot frailer than I'd expected."

"She walks up to the shops and back, and I take her to the park sometimes. She likes that, especially when all the flowers are out. And sometimes we go on the bus to the cemetery.

"Don't look like that — it's not being morbid. She loves to sit up there — she says she enjoys the peace and quiet, and the view over the city."

Matt was thoughtful as he parked the car.

"You'll have more of an idea than me of Auntie Em's likes and dislikes," he said as they chose a trolley.

"Not that she eats much," Alison said, "but she's not too keen on curry, I know that."

Matt watched her pick up and examine a cauliflower.

"You have beautiful hands," he said. He couldn't help it.

She stared at him blankly.

"Do you mind?" she hissed, and he grinned cheerfully at her.

"Not a bit."

When they arrived back with the shopping, Emily noticed Alison's face was slightly flushed. Her sharp eyes could detect no change in her nephew's calm, though.

When Matt suggested Alison should stay to have the meal with them, Emily gave up her kitchen with good grace.

The atmosphere seemed to thaw as the cooking progressed. There was a lot of laughter, and Emily was pleasantly surprised by the excellent meal they produced.

Matt insisted on seeing Alison home later that evening, and Emily noted that, despite her protests, she surrendered gracefully.

The next few weeks were happy ones for Emily. Matt took her to all the places she used to take him to when he was a lad, and others she had never been to before.

She even enjoyed walking, as long as it wasn't too far, knowing she would have a strong arm to lean on if her legs got too tired.

One Sunday they all went for a picnic on the moors. It was still a bit chilly, but they found a sheltered spot out of the wind.

Matt had put a reclining chair in the boot and, after they had eaten, he and Alison left Emily dozing happily in the sunshine while they went for a walk.

"It's beautiful up here, isn't it?" she said, leading the way through the bracken.

"Great," Matt agreed, taking deep breaths of fresh air.

"Race you to the top!" She laughed, taking off at a speed she

Enjoy Great Reading Every Week!

IF you've enjoyed this Annual, you're sure to love "The People's Friend" magazine.

Every week there are romantic and heartwarming Stories and compelling Serials. Knitting, craft and cookery are popular regular features. Also included are photofeatures from all corners of Britain, gardening tips, doctor's advice, readers' own contributions, special offers and competitions — even a page just for children.

For information about subscription rates, ask your local newsagent, or write to: Subscribers Dept., "The People's Friend", 80 Kingsway East, Dundee DD4 8SL.

163

couldn't sustain as they struggled up the steep hill.

At the top, the wind nearly blew them over, but the view was worth it. They sat down and as she turned a smiling face to his, he leaned forward and gently removed her glasses.

"Why do you hide those lovely eyes behind these things?"

She flushed.

"Maybe you've just been hiding behind them." His voice was gentle. He smiled and kissed her nose before putting the glasses gently back behind her ears. Then he put an arm round her shoulders.

"To stop you blowing away." He laughed, and she leaned against him, warm and happy in his closeness.

OVER those weeks, Emily watched Alison bloom.

The dark hair was soon allowed to frame her face, and the glasses were replaced by contact lenses. She started choosing clothes according to the colours Matt liked. It was a lovely summer — she never wanted it to end.

One evening, Alison and Matt were washing up in the kitchen while Emily watched the ITV news.

"I'm off tomorrow," Matt said.

Alison let a plate slip through her hands into the soapy water, and her stomach lurched.

"I've got to visit my sisters to see the little nephews and nieces for the first time. I'll be gone a couple of weeks."

He put an arm round her, and grinned.

"Will you miss me?"

Alison swallowed the lump in her throat and kept her eyes on the washing-up bowl.

"I'm sorry, Ally — that wasn't fair. What I really want to say is — I'll miss you. My darling, sweet, lovely Ally."

He turned her to face him and lifted her chin with a finger.

"I've fallen in love with you. You must know that — the way I've been behaving. If you don't, perhaps this will help to convince you."

He bent to kiss her — a deep, long kiss. Alison didn't even feel the soapy water trickling down her arms as she lifted them to hold him close.

When Emily came out of the living-room, the kitchen door was open and she saw the two figures melted into one. She tiptoed quietly back.

While Matt was away, she spoke to Alison.

"I think you're in love with Matthew. Am I right?"

"I think so, too." Alison's face lit up. "To be honest, I don't know what's happened to me. I've never felt like this before!"

"Well, I don't have to ask him if he's in love with you. It's as plain as the nose on my face." Emily paused. "If he asks you to go back to Australia with him, will you go?"

"I think I'd follow him to the ends of the earth."

A Century of Change

Look To The Future

MODERN technology has changed all of our lives during the 20th century.

Gone are the days when housework meant scrubbing and polishing for hours and never being free of work. New gadgets save time and effort. Washing machines, tumble driers, dish washers, microwaves, food processors, vacuums — even the humble kettle — all make life easier in the home.

We can also rely on a safe, efficient transport network.

Cable and satellite technology linked to our TV sets has given us access to an ever-increasing range of entertainment and information services. We can even phone directly to the other side of the world.

Go to book a cinema ticket or a holiday and all the information you require will be called up at the touch of a button on a computer.

Personal computers are now a feature of many homes and open up a whole new world of fun and learning.

It is the Internet which should take us into the 21st century. Perhaps in years to come, you'll be doing your shopping, chatting to your friends or even catching up on the latest "Friend" Serials, all at a touch of a button!

•••••• 1990 – 2000 ••••••

Spectrum.

After she'd gone, Emily stood at the sink, rinsing out the cups. She glanced out of the window. It was always dark looking across the back yard to the high brick wall and the looming gasworks.

Each time she looked out of this window, she tried to imagine a different scene: a coral beach, palm trees and a turquoise sea, or rolling plains leading to snow-capped mountains . . .

Now she tried to imagine the red, sandy outback, gum trees, kangaroos and koala bears.

Suddenly she felt a wave of loneliness sweep over her. If Alison left . . .! She tried not to think about it.

It hadn't been so bad when she'd had Smokey, but there was so much

165

traffic about these days, she'd be reluctant to have another cat. And she did miss the soothing presence of a cat in her lap . . .

Two weeks later, Matt returned. It was odd how just one other person seemed to fill the little house to bursting point. But in the next few days, he spent quite a lot of time away, and when Emily asked what he'd been up to, he would smile mysteriously and say nothing.

Then, one morning when they were sitting having elevenses, Matt leaned forward with a serious look on his face.

"You must be very attached to this little house, having lived here so long, Auntie Em."

"Well, things have changed a lot since I moved in," Emily remarked. "There were no cars in the street for a start. It was quiet, too . . ."

HOW would you feel about moving?" Matt said cautiously, and she snorted.

"At my age? I can't see that happening. No — I don't think I'll be going anywhere, dear. You'll be off home soon, and I don't want you worrying about me. I'm fine here."

"That's just it, Auntie Em. I'm not going back to Australia — I've made up my mind. For quite a while I've been hankering after soft drizzle on my face, crisp frosty mornings, and a good old fog! If you can understand that."

Emily smiled.

"I know," he went on, "that Alison would come with me if I wanted to go back. We've talked it through. You know I love her, don't you? She's the best thing that's happened to me.

"But I've been looking around for somewhere to buy. I've got a bit of money saved, and I wanted a job I could do outdoors.

"Well, I've found this great place. It's a market-garden business with hothouses, and fifteen acres."

"How wonderful!" Emily exclaimed with delight, turning away slightly to hide the sudden shine of tears in her eyes.

"The thing is, if you were interested, there's room for you, too. If you felt like living in the country, that is."

Emily was stunned.

"I'm not putting this very well, am I?" Matt groaned. "I've asked Alison to marry me, and we'd be really pleased if you'd come and live with us. You'd have your own rooms.

"But —" he bent forward "— we want you to make up your own mind." He grinned.

"I don't know what to say." Emily felt bemused.

"At least come out with us tomorrow to have a look at it — won't you?"

"Yes, dear. I'd like that."

The next day was fine with a light breeze — a real spring day.

Matthew drove his new car — much more comfortable, to Emily's mind — out of town for half an hour before turning off the main road.

They passed through two small villages before Matt turned into a drive. To one side were half a dozen large greenhouses and some outbuildings.

As they passed one, Emily caught sight of what she thought might be Matt's old car. A tractor was ploughing on the other side of the hedge, and the driver waved his hand.

Matt pulled up in front of the house.

"This is it," he said. "Hilltop." He helped Emily out of the car, and Alison took her arm.

"This way." She walked her round the corner of the house.

A ground-floor extension had been built on at the back, and they walked up to the door. Matt unlocked it, and motioned them through.

"Bedroom, bathroom, kitchen and —" he waved an arm "— living-room."

All the doors were open. His voice echoed in the emptiness.

The living-room was spacious, with a large picture window. It contained a broken tea chest, some pieces of newspaper, and an old chair with the stuffing oozing out.

"Hello," Emily said to the occupant of the chair, and the tabby cat opened one eye and leapt on to the windowsill.

Alison reached forward to put a hand on her arm.

"I think you'd like it here, Auntie Em," she said quietly. "You don't mind if I call you that, do you? I feel as if you've been a real auntie to me."

Emily patted her hand.

"It doesn't look much now, but we'd do it up properly, of course. And you'd bring all your own stuff with you."

"We'll let you have a look around on your own, if you like . . ." Matt said softly.

Emily nodded.

"Won't be long," Alison said.

Emily sat down in front of the window. An unkempt lawn, liberally dotted with daisies and dandelions, sloped down to a hedge and a stream. There were sheep grazing in the field beyond.

A patchwork of fields, spinneys and woodland stretched to the hills in the distance.

I'll be able to watch the sun set over the hills, she thought, and she felt her heart would burst with joy.

The cat jumped down from the window and padded towards her. It looked up, summing her up carefully, before leaping on to her lap. It turned around a few times before settling down. She stroked its head and scratched behind its ears, and it began to purr.

If I were a cat, she thought, watching the sun dance on the ripples of the stream, I'd be purring, too . . . ❏

NATALIE RICHARDS wanted to skip with pleasure on her way down to the bus station with her mother. She usually did, dancing along the pavement at the end of her mother's restraining hand. This morning, in her big warm winter boots, she had to move more sedately but still, inside, she had the same excited feeling that made her legs twitch.

She had woken early remembering at once that toda she was going into town wit Mum — just the two of them Dad was taking Jack round t play with one of his friends.

It would be a long journey b bus from the suburbs right int the centre of London, but muc more fun than the underground.

"You can't see anything! Natalie would complain if the took the tube.

They always did the same things on their special days out together. They'd shop for whatever was needed, maybe go to a museum, and then they'd have tea somewhere before they came home by another long and exciting bus ride.

Natalie had planned out the whole day but when she'd opened her eyes that morning, something unexpected had happened.

Natalie's

BIG DAY OUT

by Kate Hardstaff

Illustration by Melvyn Warren-Smith.

"A late fall of snow! Nearly Easter and it's snowing!"

Natalie had heard her mother's exclamation as she pattered downstairs in her dressing-gown.

"You'll need your winter woollies today!" Natalie was told.

So Natalie was well wrapped up as they made their way through the light slush on the pavements.

A small huddle of people was waiting by the stop, grumbling about having to stand in the cold, waiting for the driver.

"We need to bring back the old buses," said an elderly man. "No standing about then while the driver had his cup of tea."

Natalie gazed up at him.

"I expect he needs it though, doesn't he, after driving all that way?" she suggested, trying to be helpful. "My nana always says there's nothing quite like a nice cup of tea." Unconsciously, she imitated her nana's tone and the man gave a wry chuckle.

At that moment, the driver emerged from the office nearby, foam cup in hand, as though he'd heard them.

"Let me open up the bus for you so you can wait in comfort."

The elderly man was pleased. But Natalie, still tracing careful circles in the snow with the toe of her boot, would have liked to stand outside a while longer, catching the last few sleety flakes.

The Reluctant Cat

MY cat would not go out today —
He thought it far too chilly.
I tried to haul him off the chair
And told him he was silly.

But he would not budge at all
And clung on to the chair.
He looked at me in anguish.
"It's much too cold out there."

I tried to pick my feline up
But the chair hung on below.
This cat, he did not relish
A trip into the snow.

I tried to trick him outwards
With food, but he's not daft,
He curled up in a little ball
And probably he laughed.

Eventually I found a way —
I took him for a ride.
While cat sat there indignantly
I wheeled the chair outside!
— *Enid Pearson.*

NATALIE moved on quickly, though, to the next excitement. Could they get the seat upstairs right at the front? As soon as her mother had shown the driver their passes, she was off up the stairs.

When her mother joined her, Natalie was leaning forward in the front seat, her nose almost against the window.

"Are we going soon?" she demanded.

"Is everyone on the bus?" asked her mother.

"Almost everyone. There's an old lady with a young lady and that's almost all."

Soon, they heard a commotion on the stairs and a soft voice.

"Mum, you can't possibly. Look, there's a seat just there, by the doors."

"Oh, the seats for old ladies like me? I'm not sitting in a draught all the way to Trafalgar Square!" exclaimed a strong elderly voice. "I want to see where we're going. You take my stick and I'll be fine on the stairs."

The bus driver waited patiently while the footsteps came slowly up. Natalie knew that the driver could see upstairs because there was a mirror at the front. She'd peered down it sometimes but she couldn't see the driver so she didn't understand how it worked.

"Oh, look!" the voice said with obvious pleasure. "The front seat's vacant. We'll sit there, Joyce."

"Oh, Mum, you're just like a —" Joyce saw Natalie sitting, bright-eyed, watching her, and stopped hastily. Being a child wasn't such a bad thing, after all, she thought suddenly, as the little girl smiled at the elderly lady.

"It's a good view up here, isn't it?" The older woman's tone was confidential.

Natalie nodded, mouth tucked into a little smile.

The double decker pulled away at last and Vera Stewart leaned back in her seat. Her daughter had been right: it was ridiculous for a woman her age to climb up to the top deck of a bus. But then, what were days out for?

Vera turned now and patted her daughter's knee.

"Never mind, dear, when you're my age, you can be as cantankerous as you like, too!"

They smiled at each other in complete understanding.

VERA sat and watched the familiar streets go by, enjoying every new sight. She enjoyed, too, the excitement of the little girl opposite. She'd been that age when she'd first made the journey into London, from a suburb then still like a village.

The rooftops were still tipped with snow as the bus rumbled slowly onward, deeper into the centre. The last few gardens were disappearing and those that remained belonged to very grand properties.

Vera studied the rose garden in one, bare and quiet at this time of year but beautifully laid out, and thought of how Jack would have approved of it. Then she realised that, almost for the first time, she'd thought of him with a smile and not a tear.

The traffic was increasing around them and Natalie leaned back in her seat with delight as they pulled up in a long queue at the traffic lights.

"We're going to swallow up the car in front, I know we are," she whispered dramatically to her mother, as the tall front of the bus hid the car ahead from her sight.

Joyce shared a smile with Natalie's mother who was only glancing through her newspaper. She, too, had brought something to read, but her mother's interest in the passing world was infectious. In the end, book on her lap, Joyce simply gazed out of the windows, too.

As the bus rolled into Baker Street, Vera began remembering the old days.

"There used to be a bank there at one time . . . a tea room there where I met your father for lunch . . ."

By now, the foursome in the front seats felt like old-timers compared to the passengers who were only getting on for a couple of stops.

NATALIE'S mother told them about their day out and Natalie herself joined in.

"My brother Jack is playing with his friend today and Daddy's at work so I get Mum all to myself."

"Jack . . ." Vera repeated and Natalie's mother was surprised to see the old lady's lips quiver slightly even as she smiled.

"My husband's name was Jack, too," she said, after a moment. "The old names come back into fashion, don't they?"

"Yes," said Natalie's mother gently, noticing the past tense the lady had used. "It's still a fine name."

And they smiled at each other for a moment.

As Selfridges came up on their left, Natalie's mother was gathering up their things.

"We'll start here," she said. "A new summer dress, I think." She smiled down at Joyce and Vera as she stood up. "How silly to buy summer dresses in the snow!"

The little girl turned reluctantly away from her treasured front seat at last as the bus stopped.

Vera, seeing her slow steps, smiled.

"Never mind — you've got the whole journey back to look forward to!" she said, and was rewarded by Natalie's beaming smile.

Vera and Joyce stayed on the bus until it reached Trafalgar Square.

"Tea first, I think," Vera suggested to Joyce as they climbed down the steps. "What a shame —"

"— the Lyons Corner House isn't still there!" Joyce finished for her with a laugh.

Vera smiled.

"Then a stroll through the Embankment Gardens."

Her daughter agreed.

"It's your day," she said.

"Yes," said Vera, and set out to enjoy it thoroughly.

They got on the homeward bus at the Aldwych and Joyce didn't protest when her mother set off up the stairs to the front.

They turned at Oxford Circus, catching up with another bus in front as they did so.

People waiting at the stop were milling about on the crowded pavement, trying to decide which bus to get on.

Vera, leaning to look down on the heads, saw a bright coat and a little girl in warm winter boots. With her stick, she knocked, loudly and imperiously, on the window and saw people glance up in response.

The little girl's head tilted up, and her face lit with a smile. She tugged at her mother's hand urgently, pulling her back from the platform of the bus in front.

Moments later, Natalie and her mother appeared.

"Hello! Did you have a nice day out? We had a lovely time!" Natalie cried. "I wanted to stay, but Mum said we had to get back before the — rush hour."

Vera nodded.

"Joyce said just the same to me."

"What did you do today?" Natalie asked, with interest.

"We went for tea. Then we went for a walk through the gardens along the river. We did a little shopping . . ." It didn't sound very exciting as she told it, but Natalie nodded solemnly and explained how they, too, had had tea and done some shopping.

"And we went to a museum where they had Egyptian things," Natalie related importantly. "They were ever so old but there was a tea-set just like mine!"

Joyce tried hard not to laugh, but Vera nodded very seriously in return.

The two voices murmured on while Vera's daughter and Natalie's mother looked quietly out of their separate windows. They were both tired; it had been a long day and they each had to get their charges home, fed and quietened down.

After a while, the voices were softer and, as they came into the suburbs once more, Natalie's mother felt a movement and looked round. Her daughter's head was lolling gently against her shoulder, eyes closed.

She looked across and caught Joyce's eye.

Vera, still sitting upright with a straight back, had her eyes closed, too, swaying gently with the rhythm of the bus.

The two women smiled over the sleeping heads at each other. It had been a good day out for them all. ❑

Printed and Published in Great Britain by D. C. Thomson & Co., Ltd., Dundee, Glasgow and London. © D. C. Thomson & Co., 1999. While every reasonable care will be taken, neither D. C. Thomson & Co., Ltd., nor its agents wil accept liability for loss or damage to colour transparencies or any other material submitted to this publication.

ISBN 0-85116-708-X
EAN 9-780851-167084

Loughrigg Tarn And The Langdale Pikes, The Lake District

IT'S not hard to see why Wordsworth loved the Lake District, and the scenery which inspired him is still a delight to discover. Visitors can tour his old home — Dove Cottage in Grasmere — to learn more about the man and his poetry.

The landscape remains almost unchanged from the days Wordsworth enjoyed wandering "lonely as a cloud" through these lovely hills and dales. High peaks, with remote tarns nestling below them, send out a call which reaches the hearts of thousands every year.